MONTANA SPACES

About the Montana Land Reliance

The Montana Land Reliance, which sponsored *Montana Spaces*, conserves ecologically and agriculturally significant land as a living resource for present and future generations. The combination of wide-open spaces, abundant wildlife, and world-renowned trout fisheries make Montana a national treasure. Because ecosystems do not begin and end at fencelines, both private citizens and public agencies must be good stewards of their lands if these resources are to survive.

Development pressures on lands surrounding Yellowstone National Park—our oldest, largest national park—constitute the greatest threat to the wellbeing of its wildlife. Today the Montana Land Reliance holds permanent conservation easements on 54,000 acres; nearly half of these protected private lands lie within the Greater Yellowstone Ecosystem. It is an important beginning.

To learn more about this private conservation effort and what you can do to help, please write the Montana Land Reliance, P.O. Box 355, Helena, MT 59624, or phone (406) 443-7027.

Emma Joy Dana made the handsome wood engravings that grace the openings of each chapter.

MONTANA SPACES

*Essays and Photographs
in Celebration of Montana*

Edited and with an Introduction by
WILLIAM KITTREDGE

Photographs by JOHN SMART

Lyons & Burford, Publishers

Printed in the United States of America

10 9 8 7 6 5 4 3

Library of Congress Cataloging-in-Publication Data

Montana spaces.

  Bibliography: p.
  1. Montana—Social life and customs. 2. Montana—
Description and travel—1981–   —Views. I. McGuane,
Thomas. II. Smart, John, 1947–   . III. Kittredge,
William, 1932–   .
F731.M757 1988   978.6   88–27384
ISBN 1–55821–094–6

The Montana Land Reliance wishes to extend its heartfelt thanks to:

Camille and William S. Broadbent

and

Consuelo and Seth Low Pierrepont

for financial support that made the special portfolio of photographs by John Smart possible.

CONTENTS

Photographic insert follows page 158

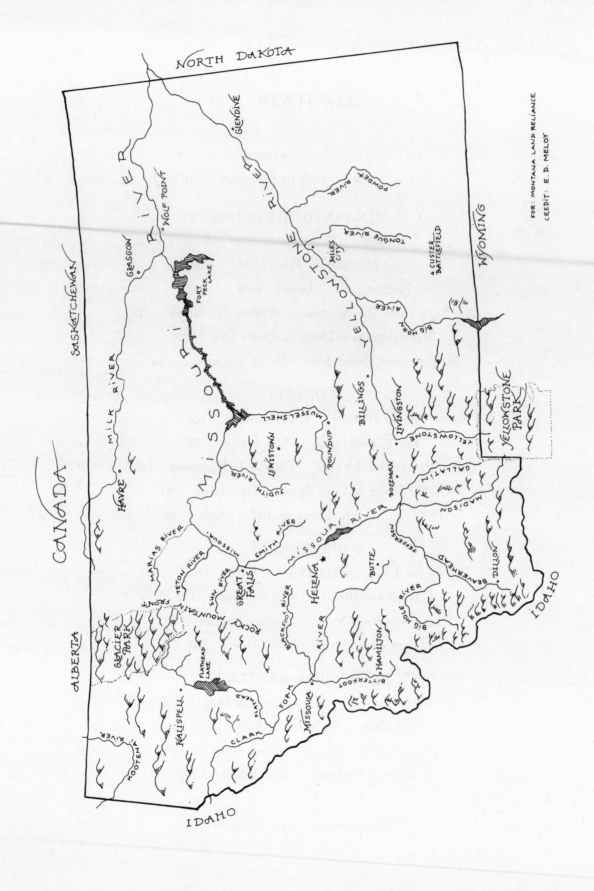

PREFACE

This is a book about Montana; it is only indirectly about the Montana Land Reliance. To commemorate Montana's Statehood Centennial, the Montana Land Reliance commissioned a series of photographic scenes and invited significant writers to express their connection to and conception of Montana. John Smart and the authors have graciously donated their original work to the Reliance.

Until the 1850s, Americans were convinced that the West was the Great American desert, forever the domain of Indians and wild animals. But by the middle of the century, rugged entrepreneurs—the fur trappers and missionaries—unlocked the West's secret wealth. The rush was on. Montana absorbed cattlemen, miners, and timbermen; by 1889 Montana had become a state.

Precious metals, timber, and open range lured people to Montana before statehood. Now people come to mine Montana's big sky horizon, not yet a man-made skyline. In Montana, Manhattan is that small agricultural community on the way to Bozeman. Yet those who come from the other Manhattan and from other urban areas in and out of Montana

JAN KONIGSBERG

for second-home retreats often exploit the big sky with a single-minded purposiveness that is as injurious as ill-conceived clearcutting, stripmining, overgrazing, and sodbusting. The proliferation of subdivisions destroys the very qualities that bring urban refugees to this part of the world.

A group of ranchers and farmers concerned about the subdivision of Montana's rich river valleys, where productive ranches are ploughed under and resurrected in a checkerboard of ranchettes, founded the Reliance in 1978. As a private, nonprofit organization, they reasoned that the Reliance could preserve the public benefits of open spaces in private ownership.

That was ten years ago. Today the Reliance has made its mark on the landscape, although the mark is invisible from the roadside. Driving Montana's blue highways, the traveler passes some unusual roadway artifacts, including arrowhead-shaped route markers and white crosses attending the scene of fatal accidents—all surrounded by the texture of space and landscape. Bullets have perforated some of the signs into colanders where an infinite background leaks into a finite foreground. Except for the barbed-wire fences, the presence of man is barely detectable. Many take solace in the open space and not a few are disturbed by it. None contest its power.

Montana remains one of the few states with relatively intact and healthy ecosystems. These nurture the most extensive trout and big-game populations in the lower 48. Many states endure enormous costs from the despoliation of their natural environment; it is far less costly to protect a healthy environment than to heal a sickly one. Through the use of perpetual conservation easements, where ranchers and farmers have donated their nonagricultural development rights to the Reliance, the Reliance has already provided conservation insurance for more than 54,000 acres of environmentally sensitive ground at a cost of less than $25 per acre.

Much of what Reliance conservation easements protect is the fertile bottom land of Montana's major river valleys. These are the riparian

x

areas that are the centers of biological diversity in the Great American desert. These areas are the source of what the biologist Paul R. Ehrlich calls "free ecosystems services." When the riparian system is degraded through insensitive land use, fish and wildlife habitat is lost, water quality deteriorates, and aesthetic and recreational opportunities decline.

Montana's streams and rivers make sense of her geography, give relief to her topography, and define her settlements. People do not inhabit Montana as such; they inhabit the Madison Valley, the Bitterroot Valley, and the Gallatin Valley. At least for now, Montana, as William Kittredge writes, "is a place knowable in human terms, where you can walk around like a citizen in a recognizable community."

People settle in Montana. Kittredge warns that settling in Montana can be dangerous if it leads to isolation, cultural aloofness, and, finally, to spiritual blindness. Yet he thinks that settlement is crucial to art. "Art has a much greater chance if it starts in a particular place, like Oxford in Mississippi and moves out toward the Nobel Prize." Tom McGuane suggests that there really is no other choice; "drive into town or stand out on I-90 and watch our nation cycle through these placeless arteries; it's there that you confront the true horror of the other option."

By no means is living in Montana all bread and roses, but it is a life beneficially affected by natural processes. The abundant and free ecosystem services in Montana depend on wise use of the land. Montana's public land holdings are immense, but private land controls the destiny of the riparian areas, upon which a substantial portion of the fish and wildlife populations depend.

The quality of the public's fresh-water resource depends upon the quality of private land management through which the public water flows. Private land provides critical elk winter range and year-round range for moose, deer, and antelope. Private land is also home to waterfowl, raptors, and many other wildlife species. The public's aesthetic and recreational enjoyment of its public resources, whether for hunting, fishing, camping or sight-seeing, depends upon private land stewardship. If elk winter range is subdivided, there will be fewer elk to hunt on the public lands. If trout spawning and rearing habitat is destroyed by insensitive private land management, there will be no wild trout fishing for the public to enjoy. And if residential subdivisions proliferate along the river banks, the public enjoyment of river recreation will be diminished.

For now there is still much left to enjoy. This book celebrates Montana today in the hope that there will be just as compelling a reason to celebrate one hundred years from now.

JAN KONIGSBERG
Montana Land Reliance

INTRODUCTION
William Kittredge

Montana has had a long run of luck with writers, from Lewis and Clark to Charlie Russell, Bud Guthrie, Stegner, Dorothy Johnson, Richard Hugo, Norman Maclean, James Welch, Ivan Doig, Tom McGuane, Jim Crumley, and David Quammen. And a string of others who aren't so famous, Nicholas Point and Nanny Alderson and Teddy Blue Abbott and Grace Stone Coates and Frank Linderman and Myron Brinig and Joseph Kinsey Howard and D'Arcy McNickle and Dan Cushman and Mildred Walker.

And others more obscure. See what you can find in your local library by Pearl Price Roberstson. See if you can find a book called *Snake Tracks* by Blaine Allen Goyins. Or *U Bet* by John Barrows. Or *At Home in the Wilderness* by John Keast Lord, or *The Old Man's Garden* by Annora Brown. If you can't find something to like in those books, you don't like much.

And then there are the great, and for most of us unknown, unexamined traditions of Native American rhetoric and storytelling. At least parts of eleven tribes live on seven reservations in Montana, and they all have ancient, distinctive literatures. See if your library has a copy of *Stories of the White Clay People* by the Gros Ventre Elders at Fort

Belknap, or *Blackfoot Texts*, stories gathered around Browning just after 1900 by an anthropologist named Uhlenbeck, with the help of James Tatsey. In your attention to such texts, a world will begin to come open.

The westering movement always drew storytelling adventurers. And we can understand the impulse. Men without women to appreciate them, living lives of what they clearly understood to be at least partways high adventure, the day ended—like anybody else, they wanted to understand and celebrate themselves. So they told what stories they knew and made up some more, about themselves.

In *The Journal of a Trapper, or Nine Years in the Rocky Mountains, 1834–1843*, Osborne Russell tells us "The long winter evenings were passed away by collecting in some of the most spacious lodges and entering into debates, arguments or spinning 'long yarns until midnight, in perfect good humor, and I for one will cheerfully confess that I have derived no little benefit from the frequent arguments and debates held in what we called 'The Rocky Mountain College,' and I doubt not that some of my comrades who considered themselves classical scholars added to their wisdom in the assemblies, however rude they might appear."

Imagine that stinking assemblage of ghostly legendary figures, men like Bridger and Jedediah Smith, more than a thousand miles upriver from the nearest town, as they defined themselves in their narratives. They were part of a tradition ancient as campfires.

And by the latter half of the nineteenth century such figures, their tall tales and hero stories, had emerged from the shadowy enclaves of nighttime folk-narrative. Their stories were written down. We all know about Mike Fink and Paul Bunyan. The production of such stories became literary cottage industry. Legend has it there were some 1,700 nickel/dime novels written about Buffalo Bill. And hundreds more about Wild Bill Hicock and Calamity Jane.

A young newspaper man changed his public name to Mark Twain, a tag connected to the adventuring enterprise of riverboating on the Mississippi, and went west from Missouri to the gold fields of California. He wrote a lot of mostly nonsensical tales about gold-field life, culminating in a book called *Roughing It*, and found himself a literary success in the East Coast cities of America, where the hunger for hero-stories seemed insatiable. And then he transcended all that, and wrote a great book, *Huckleberry Finn*. Samuel Clemens of Missouri had gone out to the adventuring world and listened carefully to the cadences of those ironically inventive, so insistently boyish and heartbroken storytelling voices, and he knew treasure when he heard it.

The voices he heard probably sounded a lot like Charlie Russell, who was the natural, the cowboy painter who got it right and traded his famous paintings for drinks and told it like it was. This, for instance, is supposed to be a true story. In the early 1920s a group of booster citizens from Great Falls threw a celebration in honor of themselves. Russell was asked to speak. After listening to a long run of windy bombast, he finally got his chance:

> In my book a pioneer is a man who turned all the grass
> upside down, strung bob-wire over the dust that was left,
> poisoned the water and cut down the trees, killed the
> Indian who owned the land, and called it progress. If I
> had my way, the land here would be like God made it,
> and none of you sons of bitches would be here at all.

There is likely a good deal of truth in that story. I got it from K. Ross Toole, a historian who was all his life troubled by the fact that he was by nature another legendary storyteller. Ross wore the constraints of his profession with some difficulty, but he swore that was an actual transcript of Russell's little speech. Even if it's not verbatim, it sounds like Russell, and it ought to be true. In "The Man Who Shot Liberty Valance," Dorothy Johnson has a frontier newspaper man say "Print the legend."

Another tradition got going in the early 1920s, when H. G. Merriam started the second creative-writing program in the nation (Harvard was first) at the University of Montana. A few years later he founded the first literary magazine in the West, *Frontier*, later *Frontier and Midland*. The influence of both the writing program and the magazine was important to the literature of the American West. Bud Guthrie and Wallace Stegner published their first stories in *Frontier and Midland*.

In 1964, Leslie Fiedler left Montana and moved his considerable reputation to the State University of New York in Buffalo. In the fall of that year Richard Hugo came to replace Fiedler and teach at the University of Montana.

Fiedler had been both revered and despised. A great teacher and controversial personality, he encouraged students to read with rigorous engagement, and to love writing worthy of such examination. Like Merriam before him, Fiedler influenced Montana people to understand art as real and important in their lives; like Merriam, Fiedler performed a great service.

If you travel in Montana you will meet people who will tell you about their days studying with Merriam or Fiedler as if they were talking about a golden age. These are people who were taught to love books and ideas, and they are one of Montana's prime humanistic resources. But in the fall of 1964 Merriam was an old man, and Fiedler was gone.

It is easy to imagine Dick Hugo's uneasiness; he was forty years old, with a Masters Degree earned while studying under Theodore Roethke at the University of Washington, and two well-reviewed books of poetry, *A Run of Jacks* and *Death of the Kapowsin Tavern*. But he had spent the prior thirteen years working for Boeing in Seattle, and he had never taught. "I was scared to death," Hugo said.

Then Montana had some more good luck: Hugo turned out to be a man come to the right place at the right time. While suffering the traumas detailed in "The Milltown Union Bar," his marriage broken, drinking hard, Hugo was also searching out solace along the backroads of Montana, and, in his way, he was finding it. Hugo was a highly sophisticated literary modernist, and literary modernism is if nothing else a set of techniques designed to help us see the world and its possibilities in fresh ways.

In a very real sense Hugo reinvented the possibilities for literature in

Montana for an oncoming generation. In poems like "Degrees of Gray in Phillipsburg" (1966) Hugo proved that Montana, like anywhere, could be understood as a place resonating with significance, and that high art was as possible in Montana as in Paris or New York or anywhere.

Hugo underlined this in a number of ways. He was well thought of and well connected in national literary circles, and his fine poems about Montana were soon showing up in nationally important magazines like *The New American Review* and *The New Yorker*. And they were being taken seriously by critics. Hugo also introduced his students to editors, and helped them get their first works published.

All this was of course enormously heartening to young people dickering with the idea of making literary careers in the provincial backlands of the Northern Rockies. Maybe it *was* possible to make a serious run at the world from a home base in Montana. Within a couple of years a remarkably talented group had gathered in Hugo's classes, taking strength from this man who convinced them that writing well about places and people they loved was not only an important and vital way to spend their lives, but also a possible route to success.

And Hugo, although he was no doubt the prime mover, was not alone. Earl Ganz came in 1966, to direct the Creative Writing Program. James Crumley came that same year, to teach fiction writing, and Madeline De Frees came soon after, to teach poetry writing.

When I came to Missoula in 1969, I found a remarkable creative community centered at the University, and that community sustained and sheltered me, as it did so many others—James Welch, Rick DeMarinis, Pat Todd, Ed Lahey, Annick Smith, Denise Scanlon, Roger Dunsmore, Wayne Ude, Michael Moon, Dave Thomas, Roberta Hill Whiteman, David Long, Bob Wrigley, Andrew Grossbardt, Bob Reid, Paul Zarzyski, Ralph Beer, Sandra Alcosser, Beth Ferris, Kurt Duecker, Jon Davis, Nancy Hunter, Linda Weasel Head, Peter Bowen, Ripley Schemm, and Mathew Hansen.

Another community began to form when Tom McGuane decided to

settle near the fishing waters in Paradise Valley south of Livingston. McGuane is a man with a considerable gift for drawing his friends around him, people like William Hjortsberg and Richard Brautigan and Tim Cahill.

And, in Bozeman, we have David Quammen and Greg Keeler and Patricia Henley. And at Fort Peck, Bill Yellow Robe.

And Wally McRae and Spike Van Cleve and Mary Blew and Bill Stockton. And Richard Ford and Jon Jackson.

And hold your horses.

At this point, getting close to the present, there's too much, too many names, and I am reduced to such lists, which I detest. But even the lists are obvious good news.

If you wanted to know why I live in Montana, I would tell you it was because Montana is the place where I feel most securely connected to luck. By luck I mean all these writers and so many more, and a history of their serious and quite political attention to the well-being of the place where we live.

In Montana we have a society I can understand on a human scale, which encourages me to feel like I can take part any time I choose to participate, as a writer, and have an impact if I say anything worth hearing. I think a lot of our writers feel the same way. This book is proof of that. These writers are saying this place we live in is valuable, to be cherished.

We must thank them by taking good care.

1 COMING INTO THE COUNTRY

RUNOFF

Thomas McGuane

The fishing life in Montana produces a particular apprehension that affects fishermen like a circadian rhythm: irrational dread of runoff. Early spring is capable of balmy days; and though the water is cold, the rivers are as benign as brooks in dreams, their pools and channels bright and perfect. But year-round experience shows that in short order they will be buried in snowmelt and irrigation waste, and their babied low-water contours will disappear under the hoggish brown rush. Once runoff begins, the weather is often wonderful. The canopies of cottonwood open like green umbrellas. But it can be a long wait before the rivers clear, a wait so long it seems possible to lose track of the whole idea.

In early spring, it is time to begin when friends say, "I know I should get out. I just haven't had the time." Here is the chance to steal a march, to exercise those fish whose memory has been dulled by the long winter. Crazy experiments can be undertaken at this time, such as photographing a trout held in your left hand with a camera held in your right hand. Before-the-runoff is time out of time; it is the opportunity to steal fishing from an impudent year.

You can tell when you have started early enough when the first landowner whose permission you ask stares at you with zenophobic eyes. His first thought is that you are there to pilfer or harm his family. Let him examine your rod and scrutinize your eyes. The eyes of a fishermen are not so good; so keep them moving. Spot a bit of natural history and describe it. Above all, don't say that your dad and your granddad before you fished this same stretch at their pleasure. The landowner of today does not like any surprising seniority just now. He's having hell holding onto the place. Turn and go to your vehicle. Don't back to it.

A sign of real desperation for me is when I begin to tie my own flies. I once made the simple accomodation that others do this better than I do, that they are meant to fill a fly need in others. They are professional fly tyers and their monkish solitude is rendered habitable by the knowledge that their creations are helping all-thumbs types like myself drag hogs onto the gravel. But this compact with an invisible support team was something I could no longer honor by March; and I began to fill fly box after fly box with my crude elk-hair caddises, Griffith's Gnats, and Gold-ribbed Hare's Ears.

I wandered around the various forks of my home river, separated by many miles of rolling hills: one would be running off, the other clear, depending upon the exact kind of country it drained. I clambered down slick or snowy rocks to dangle my thermometer in the water. But in the spring there was, even on a snowy day, a new quality of light, as if the light had acquired richness that you could feel, that trees, grass, and animals could feel, a nutritious light coming through falling snow. There had come a turning point and now spring was more inexorable than the blizzards. I knew the minute this snow quit there would be some place I could fish.

The next morning was still and everything was melting. I went to a small river out in the foothills north of where I live. This early in the year when I drive down through a ranch yard or walk across a pasture toward the stream, my heart pounds as it has all my life for a glimpse of moving water. Moving water is the most constant passion I've had; it can be current or it can be tide; but it can't be a lake and it can't be mid-ocean where I have spent some baffled days and weeks more or less scratching my head. The river was in perfect shape, enough water that most of its braided channels were full. There were geese on the banks and they talked at me in a state of high alarm as they lifted and replaced their feet with wierd deliberation.

As soon as I got in the river, I felt how very cold the water was. Nevertheless, a few caddises skittered on top of the water. An hour later, some big gray drakes came off like a heavenly message sent on coded insects, a message that there would indeed be dry-fly fishing on earth again. I am always saying, though it's hardly my idea, that the natural state of the universe is cold; but cold-blooded trout and cold-blooded mayflies are signs of the world's retained heat, as is the angler, wading upstream in a cold spring wind in search of delight. Nevertheless, the day had opened a few F-stops at the aperture of sky, a sign and a beginning. I caught one of the mayflies and had a long look: about a number-12, olive, brown, and gray the operative colors, two-part tail. I had something pretty close in my fly box, having rejected the Red Quill and the Quill Gordon as close but no cigar.

A couple of brilliant male mergansers went overhead. They are hard on fish and despised, but their beauty is undisputed. In a short time, they would migrate out of here and I didn't know where they went. They were referred to in Lewis and Clark's journals as the red-headed fishing duck, a better name.

The river combined in a single channel where the volume of water produced a steady riffle of two or three feet of depth. I started where it tailed out and worked my way up to where slick water fell off into the rapids. The mayflies were not in great numbers but they were carried down this slick and over the lip into the riffle. My staring magnified their plight into postcards of Niagara Falls, a bit of sympathetic fancy cancelled by the sight of swirls in the first fast water. I cast my fly straight into this activity and instantly hooked a good rainbow. It must have been the long winter's wait or the knowledge that the day could end any minute; but I desperately wanted to land this fish. I backed down out of the fast water while the fish ran and jumped; then I sort of cruised him into the shallows and got a hand on him. He was a brilliant looking fish and I thought I could detect distress in his eyes as he looked, gulping, out into midair. I slipped the barbless hook out and eased him back into the shallows. Two sharp angles and he was gone in deep green water.

It started to cloud up and grow blustery. The temperature plummeted. I went back to my truck, stripped off my waders, put up my gear, and started home, past the black old tires hung on the fenceposts with messages painted on them about cafes and no hunting. I kept thinking that the sort of sporadic hatch that had begun to occur was perfect for leisurely dry-fly fishing, if the weather had held. By the time I got to the house, it was winter again and I was trying to look up that dun, concluding for all the good it would do me, that it was *Ephemerella compar*. Even as I write this, I visualize a trout scholar in pince-nez rising up out of the Henry's Fork to correct my findings.

When you have stopped work to go fishing and then gotten weathered out, your sense of idleness knows no bounds. You wander around the house and watch the weather from various windows. From my bedroom I could see great gusts of snow, big plumes and curtains marching across the pasture. Did I really catch a rainbow on a dry fly this morning?

The next day broke off still and sunny, and spring was sucking that snow up and taking it to Yucatan. I ran into a friend of mine at the post office who had seen a young male gyrfalcon—a gyrfalcon!—hunting partridges on my place. In an hour, I was standing with my fly rod in the middle of a bunch of loose horses, looking off a bank into a deep, green-black pool where swam a number of hog rainbows. I had been there before and you couldn't approach the spot except to stand below where the slow-moving pool tailed out rather rapidly. The trouble was you had to stay far enough away from the pool that it was hard to keep your line off the tailwater that produced instantaneous drag. You needed a seven-foot rod to make the cast and a twenty-foot rod to handle the slack. They hadn't built this rod yet. It would have been a two-piece rod with a spring-loaded hinge driven by a cartridge in the handle with a flash suppressor. Many of us had been to this pool to learn why the rainbows had grown to be hogs who would never be dragged onto a gravel bar. They were going to stay where they were with their backs up and their bellies down, eating when they wanted to. I had to try it anyway and floated one up onto the pool. I got a drag-free drift of around three-eighths of an inch and went looking for another spot.

Geese and mallards flew up ahead of me as I waded, circling for altitude in the big bare tops of the cottonwoods. The air was so still and transparent you could hear everything. When the mallards circled over my head, their wingtips touched in a tense flutter and made a popping sound.

In a little back-eddy, caddises were being carried down a line of three feeding fish. I arranged for my fly to be among them, got a drift I couldn't begin to improve on, and a nice brown sucked it down. I moved up the edge of the bar to some more feeding fish. There were geese on the bar who had been ignoring me but now began to watch me and pace around. I noted one of the fish was of good size and it was feeding in a steady rhythm. I made a kind of measuring cast from my knees. The geese were getting more nervous. I made a final cast and it dropped right in the slot and started floating back to the good fish. I looked over to see what the geese were doing. The trout grabbed the fly. I looked back and missed the strike. I delivered an oath. The geese ran awkwardly into graceful flight and banked on around to the North.

This was a wonderful time to find yourself astream. You didn't bump into experts. You didn't bump into anybody. There were times when you could own this place in your thoughts as completely as a Hudson Bay trapper. The strangely human killdeer were all over the place. I considered them human because their breeding activities were accompanied by screaming fights and continuous loud bickering. When they came in for a landing, their wings set in a quiet glide while their legs ran frantically in midair. The trees in the slower bends were in a state of pickup-sticks destruction from the activity of beavers. A kingfisher flew over my head with a trout hanging from its bill. I came around a bend without alerting three more geese, floating in a backwater, sound asleep with their heads under their wings. I decided not to wake them. I ended my day right there. When I drove up out of the riverbottom in my car, I looked back to see a blue heron fishing the back eddy where I'd caught a trout. On the radio were predictions of high temperatures coming and I knew what that low-country meltoff would mean to my days on the river.

Spring was here and it was hot. In one day it shot up to the eighties. I could feel the purling melt come out from under the snowbanks. Runoff was going to drop me in midstride.

I drove away from the places that I thought would get the first dirty water, away from the disturbed ground. It was daybreak and out on the interstate I found myself in a formation of Montana Pioneers, driving Model-Ts. This piquancy didn't hold me up long and I soon made my way to a wonderful little district where various grasses, burgeoning brush, wildflowers, and blue-green strips of fragrant sage had all some-how got the news that spring had sprung. The cover was so deep in places that deer moving through it revealed only their ears, which flipped up and disappeared. An old pry bar lay lost in the grass, polished smooth by use. Ranchers never had the help they needed and they were all masters of prying; these bars had the poetry of any old tool, old dental instruments, old greasy hammers and screwdrivers around a man's work-shop, especially when the tool owner is not in immediate evidence, or dead.

The river whispered past this spot in a kind of secretive hurry. I got in and waded upstream, and sat on a small log jam to tie on a fly. The logs under me groaned with the movement of current. I was suddenly so extremely happy, the sight of this water was throwing me into such a rapturous state of mind, that I began to wonder what it could mean. I sometimes wondered if there wasn't something misanthropic in this pas-sion for solitude.

I put my thermometer into the river, knowing already it was going to come out in the 40s. Taking the temperature of the river is like taking your own temperature, the drama of the secret darkness of the interior of your mouth; you wait and wait and try to wait long enough. Is it 98.6 or am I right in thinking I don't feel too good? The water was 49°, fairly acceptable for now.

Across from my seat on the log jam was an old cabin. These old buildings along Montana trout rivers were part of their provenance, part of what came back to you, like the wooded elevations that shaped, and bent, and pushed and pulled each river so that as you tried to recreate one in your mind that winter, there was always a point you got lost, always an oxbow or meander where a kind of memory white-out occurred. I was always anxious to return to such a stretch and rescue it from amnesia.

To reach my pool, I had to wade across the riffle above the log jam and then work my way around a humongous, dead, bloated cow, inflated to a height of five feet at the ribcage. The smell was overpowering but I needed to get to that pool. There was a mule deer doe back in the trees watching me with her twin yearling fawns. One already was getting little velvet antlers.

For some reason, I was thinking how many angry people, angry faces, you saw in these romantic landscapes. It was as though the dream had backfired in isolation. There were the enraged visages behind pickup truck windshields with rifles in the back window at all seasons of the year. I remembered an old rancher telling me about a rape that had just occurred in Gardiner and in his eyes was the most extraordinary mixture of lust and rage I had ever seen. He lived off by himself in a beautiful canyon and this was the sort of thing he came up with. A friend of mine from the Midwest looked at the chairs in a restaurant covered with all the local cattle brands and cried out in despair, "Why are these people always *tooling* everything?" The pleasures of being seduced by the daily flux of the masses were not available. All the information about the world had failed to produce the feeling of the global village; the information had exaggerated the feeling of isolation. I had in my own heart the usual modicum of loneliness, annoyance, and desire for revenge; but it never seemed to make it to the river. Isolation always held out the opportunity of solitude: the rivers kept coming down from the hills.

Having reached my pool, having forded the vast stench of the cow, I was rewarded with a sparse hatch of sulphur mayflies with mottled gray wings. I caught three nice browns in a row before it shut off. I knew this would happen. A man once told me, when I asked him when you could assume a horse would ground tie and you could go off and leave him, knowing he would be there when you got back: "The horse will tell you." When I asked an old man in Alabama how he knew a dog was staunch enough to break it to stand to shot, he said, "The dog will tell you." There are times for every angler when he catches fish because the fish told him he could; and times when the trout announce they are through for the day.

Two of the most interesting fish of the next little while were fish I couldn't catch. One was on the far side of a current that ran along the side of a log. The trout was making a slow porpoising rise. I managed to reach him and he managed to rise; but drag got the fly at the instant he took and carried the fly away. The next fish I saw, another steady feeder, rose to a Light Cahill. The dinner bell at a nearby ranch house rang sharply; I looked up, the fish struck and I missed it.

I caught a nice rainbow by accident, which is the river's way of telling you that you've been misreading it. And then thunder and lightning commenced. I got out of the river. Bolting rain foretold the flood. I went up and sat under the trunk lid of my car, quite comfortably, and ate my lunch, setting a Granny Smith apple on the spare tire. The thermos of coffee seemed a boon almost to be compared to the oranges we kept on ice during the hot early weeks of bird season. The rain steadied down and I could watch two or three bends of the river and eat in a state of deep contentment. I didn't know of a better feeling than to be fishing and having enough time; you weren't so pressured that if you got a bad bank you couldn't wait until the good bank turned your way and the riffles were in the right corners. And the meal next to a stream was transforming too so that in addition to the magic apple there was the magic peanut-butter-and-jelly sandwich.

The rain stopped and I went down to where an irrigation ditch took out along a rip-rapped bank. I had a very nice Honduran cigar to smoke while I watched a heron fish the shallows. The air was still. I puffed a great cloud of smoke and it drifted across the little river; I imagined it was the ghost of my grandfather, who loved to fish. The ghost glided past the heron who ignored him politely.

I just knew something was going on. There was a readiness. The rain had barely withdrawn. The sky looked so heavy you felt if you scratched it you'd drown. This was the storm that would loose the mountain snows, and the glistening fingers of this small river system would turn brown as a farmer's hand. Time, in its most famous configuration, was "running out." It could be the storm that made runoff really get under way, my last day on the stream for a good while. One had broken out of the pattern of home life and work, and beaten inertia for the moment: might as well keep going.

I crawled down into a canyon made by the river. It was not far from where I had been fishing and the canyon was not that deep. But I needed both hands to make the descent, to lower myself from projecting roots and points of rock; and I had to throw the rod down in front of me because there was no good way to carry it. I found myself between tall cream-and-gray rock walls. The river flowed straight into dissolved chimneys, rock scours, solution holes, and fanciful stone bridges.

The sky overhead was reduced to a narrow band and the storm had reformed over that. More killdeer conducted their crazed, weeping, wing-dragging drama around my feet. The storm became ugly and I looked all around the bottom of the small canyon for a place safe to be. Lightning jumped close overhead with a roaring crack. The rain poured down, periodically lit up by the very close lightning. What little I knew about electricity made me think that bushes were a poor connection; so I burrowed into a thick clump of laurels and became mighty small, studied

THOMAS McGUANE

the laurel: round, serrated leaf, brownish yellow bark, a kind of silvery brightness from afar. It had become very gloomy. By looking at the dark mouths of the caves in the far canyon wall, I could monitor the heaviness of the rain while the steady rattle on the hood of my parka filled in the blanks. I spotted a lightning-killed tree at about my level on the far side. The river had seemed so cheerful and full of green-blue pools. Now it was all pounded white by rain and only the darker Vees of current indicated that it was anything but standing water.

Then the air pressure could be felt to lift. The dark sky broke wide open in blue. An owl crossed the river, avoiding the return of light. The rain stopped and the surface of river was miraculously refinished as a trout stream. I looked at the drops of water hanging from my fly rod. I thought of the windows of the trout opening on a new world and how appropriate it would be if one of them could see my fly.

The standing water along roadsides in spring was a wonderful thing. On the way home, I saw a flight of northern shoveller ducks, eccentric creatures in mahogany and green: and off in a pasture stock pond, teal flew and circled like butterflies unable to decide whether to land. I wondered what it was about the edges of things that is so vital, the edges of habitat, the edges of seasons, always in the form of an advent. Spring in Montana was a kind of pandemonium of release. There were certainly more sophisticated ways of taking it in than mine. But going afield with my fishing rod seemed not so intrusive and the ceremony helped, quickened my memory back through an entire life spent fishing. Besides, like "military intelligence" and "airline cuisine," "sophisticated angler" is an oxymoron. And if it weren't, it would be nothing to strive for. Angling is where the child, not the infant, gets to go on living.

It was ten minutes to five. There was absolutely no wind. I could see the corners of a few irrigation dams sticking up out of the ditches. The cottonwoods were in a blush of green. I was ready for high water.

12

CECIL MIGRATES

Ellen Meloy

Like the natural impulse that sends migratory birds over ancient corridors of flight, their way mapped by the sun and stars, the shape of a mountain or curve of river, some unmodified core of instinct for movement, a remnant of primitive human nomadism brought me to Montana. The instinct may have been aroused by celestial alignment or a subtle shift of continents. The more immediate stimuli, however, were the Army Corps of Engineers, Mickey Mouse, and a fixation with Wyoming.

One such impulse struck at a rodeo in the foothills of California's Sierra Nevada mountains. It had been a peaceful morning apart from the tarantulas mating in my bathtub and the arrival of a postcard of a road sign that said, "Lost Springs, Wyoming, population five." These omens stirred faint achings in the astrolabes of unrest. As I crossed a parking lot on the rodeo grounds, clouds of heat and dust parted to reveal the brown-and-gold Holy Grail: a Wyoming license plate with its eternally bucking horse. In the back of the truck, resting on a pile of saddles, was a cowboy.

"Take me with you," I begged. Beer from the three cups I held sloshed over my knuckles. Sweat ran down my temples and neck. In one of the world's most arid climates, my sunglasses fogged.

He was from a small town on the Tongue River near Sheridan, he said, just across the border from Montana. "Do you mind if I catch a ride?" I asked again. The idea of being able to peer over borders was appealing. Before he responded, a friend walked up and without a word traded the beers for her two-year-old son and left. I could either leave and face kidnapping charges, or stay put and babysit this short, clammy human. I stayed.

An earlier migratory urge had occurred on a cross-country road trip in the early 1970s, when I drove home to California from college on the East Coast. Two friends came along for the ride. Gas was cheap back then, and the trail into the wilderness had been broken by Lewis and Clark, Prince Maximilian of Wied, the homesteaders, Jack Kerouac, and nearly everyone else caught up in America's perpetual state of transportation. The way west was the corridor of myth and possibility. Real life was about to begin.

Our favored road costumes were secondhand, matching short-sleeved blue work shirts, the kind worn by car mechanics and hardware salesmen. Above the left breast pockets were name patches embroidered in red and white. Mine said "Cecil." The others were "Freddie" and "Dave." Although the trip journal—dubbed "Atlantis on $5 a Day"—reveals a heady savoring of the open road, our desire to be taken as serious adventurers, most capably and purposefully Lost in America, was met by a suffocating fuss. "You girls run away from home?" asked a service-station attendant only two days out. His shirt patch said "Chuck."

At a café in Cairo, Illinois, a motherly waitress told us to "scurry our sweet butts west" before the Communist invasion. The invasion was imminent, she said, because the local preacher doubled as a CIA agent. Or vice versa. Anyway, according to her, the town was full of lapsed Presbyterians gone Red. "What does a Communist look like?" Freddie asked. We cringed. The last polite inquiry about local customs from Freddie the gudgeon had grounded us in a Kentucky town for three hours with a pack of Jehovah's Witnesses. The back of our car was now filled to the armrests with copies of *The Watchtower*. Out the café window, across the street, a grinning exhibitionist caught my gaze and opened his arms and coat in a friendly Midwestern welcome. A Commie scout? Definitely the sort who invites you home to play with his animals.

Somewhere west of all the billboards and vacant lots and into the wide, dry open, my friends pined for their first sight of a cowboy. Neither had ever been west of Albany, New York. I called upon my infinitely deep reservoirs of wisdom as a westerner to prepare them for a verified sighting.

"Well," I said as we cruised across South Dakota. The summer air was fragrant with prairie grasses and buffalo bones. A copy of *The Watchtower* hung from the side window, shading the sun's copper glare. "Cowboys are slim with leathery brown faces and pale foreheads. They squint, roll cigarettes with their elbows, ride fences all day, and spit. They love horses, cattle, whoever is cooking, and women, in that order. Lifetimes spent under a broad empty sky foster keen introspection, philosophic abstraction, fierce independence, and narrative inventiveness. I for one am the very embodiment of these qualities."

Credibility waned until we spotted Ralph (so said the name on his tooled leather belt) at a truckstop outside Rapid City. He had all the cowboy accoutrements—belt, snap shirt, pointy-toed boots, sweat-stained hat—and five drooling kids and a wife with a glazed look, all jammed into an unlikely cowboy vehicle, a Volkswagen bus. We asked him to immortalize the occasion by writing in our journal. "Don't talk to strangers," he scrawled.

A journal entry from eastern Wyoming reads, "One thing worse than a sixty-foot Winnebago with a television antenna is a sixty-foot Winnebago with a television antenna and two white poodles." As I recall, this cynicism arose from a stormy night of involuntary exile from what was in those days the peaceful rusticity of state and national park campgrounds. A crowded KOA was all we could find in the downpour.

If the trumpet of doom were suddenly to sound, said South American statesman Domingo Sarmiento during his visit to this country in 1847, it would surprise two-thirds of the American population "on the roads like ants." Life at a Kampground of America on a soggy summer night in Wyoming proved that little but the technology of mobility had changed in over a century. Generators hummed, sewage hookups sloshed, a woman carrying a crock pot and a blow dryer darted puddles to the rest-room bunker. "See that pull-in over there?" the KOA attendant said, pointing to a tricycle-size slot between two gleaming aluminum Air-streams, "That'll be $8.75." Cecil, Dave, and Freddie parked the kar and kamped.

A few days later, we lingered where the Rockies lunge skyward from the Snake River Plateau at Grand Teton National Park. The camp-grounds were full when we arrived, forcing us to spend the first night on a park ranger's porch. I awoke at dawn to hear the ranger whisper in my ear, "Come with me." Fearlessly (rapists, I assumed, don't wear name tags) I followed him a mile down a trail to the edge of Jenny Lake. He dropped to his knees and reverently parted the grass to reveal a calypso orchid in full bloom.

Just as the arrival of the first cold front and a northwest wind "tells" a bird it is time to migrate south in the fall, or the taste of its ancestral river draws the salmon inland, this exquisite plant touched a migratory nerve. I stood riveted in tender agony, my fists in my mouth. Dirt en-tered my shoes, sent tentacles up my legs and through my body like a tree of stone. Beneath my feet, the tectonic plates creaked. I clodded back to camp and announced that we would follow these mountains north to Montana. But the beauty of this place unnerved my friends. Ever since St. Louis these two New Yorkers had needed things to bump into. It's too empty, they said. That's the point, I said. A vote was taken. I lost. We drove west.

The third effort to reach Montana was successful, perhaps because the migratory instinct was paired with loss of habitat. The seeds of the occasion were planted in a peculiarly western institution: the marriage between the reclamation mystique and the conspiracy of federal gov-ernment and big business to steal people's property. In the early

1960s, the citrus industry creeping northward from Los Angeles pressured the government into using the power of eminent domain to take over private land needed for irrigation projects along the Tule River as it roared out of the Sierra foothills into the San Joaquin Valley. The Army Corps of Engineers dammed the river. The reservoir behind the dam submerged the cattle ranch that had been in my family for five generations. In a state where you have to wade through 24 million immigrants from Ohio to find a native, this family goes back to primordial slime. Between the time the first ancestral molecule had homesteaded, and my childhood, the valley had gone from grazing land to dryland wheat farms, and finally to agribusiness and homogenized suburbia. California's penchant for tearing up last year's improvements for new attire obliterates its own history. It is land periodically rolled up like a carpet, out of whose ends fall condors, otters, Ishi, a neighborhood, your grandmother's house. A landscape so altered no longer sings its native notes.

I was living east of the old ranch in the last homecountry enclave deep in the Sierras when Walt Disney Productions proposed to turn the area into a 3,300-person-a-day ski resort with one nine-level plus two supplemental parking lots, ten restaurants, and twenty ski lifts. This was Phase One. It was a modest little alpine retreat capable of accommodating a visitor population twice that of a busy day at nearby Yosemite where, as every Californian and even the 507 million most recent arrivals from Ohio knew, people routinely went berserk with ocholphobia. The fear of crowds—slopes crawling with Mickey Mice on skis—was unbearable. Development had pushed me east in increments. If I continued in that direction, I would slip off the east face of the Sierras and fall into the Los Angeles Aqueduct. Surrounded, I packed up and moved to Montana. Montana, the great homing device for the restless.

Several hundred other Californians, by the way, came with me. The Bitterroot Valley, where I first lived, was full of them. Cowboy boots meticulously free of animal excreta made them easy to spot. All of them were realtors. They railed against the ruination of their former home, but imported some of its cuisine and customs. "Frost heave," one of them once lamented to me over baby vegetables in braised piglet lint dip, "is rupturing our hot tub." It's a common problem in migration. Like Cowboy Ralph in Rapid City, things aren't always what you expect.

Montana is an honest place, native cover for fugitives from large reclamation projects, decent, hardworking people, dreamers, heroes, iconoclasts, stockgrowers, and other eccentrics, native born and transplant alike. Before Alaska came along and ruined everything, one of every twenty-five square miles in America was Montanan. This much space has nurtured a healthy Cult of Place in which people find perfection, even divinity in the landscape; they finally admit that here man and earth are in the right proportion to one another.

Most people would say that an innate human instinct to migrate, lodged deep in the central nervous system, is like a tail or appendix; it's an insensible oddity whose utility died out with the hunter-gatherers. Any sense of direction we might retain comes from things like the microchip-controled digital designer compass unit on the dashboards of our BMWs. My migration instinct, though more or less confined for the last decade within Montana's borders, remains intact—blunted, perhaps, but not yet fully domesticated. The notion of home can be found in movement itself. Cecil lives.

Right now Cecil is organizing an all-out return to semi-nomadism, a culture that predates the white man's arrival here. It may in fact be the true Montana culture, a cunning strategy for the exploitation of marginal land, a true match of character and environment. "Raids are our agriculture," says a Bedouin proverb. And all those lusty Utah peach orchards to the South!

HOMESTEAD

Annick Smith

The weathered log buildings on a hillside with yellow grass would come to own me. From my first accidental sight of the place, I was hooked. I started to invent a new life. Some country family lived in the mud-chinked house with sun glinting off its tin roof, but the ranch seemed abandoned, no sounds except the humming of yellowjackets, dry grass rustling as we passed. It was an image from old photographs: rusted car bodies, random tires, and a few leghorns pecking for the last grasshoppers of summer. Home. If I lived here, who would I be?

I imagined a sturdy woman whose skin was lined as the hewn logs. She would be chopping kindling on the hard-packed dirt outside the kitchen

19

door. Her man drove a John Deere tractor along ditchbanks thick with sedge and timothy and orchard grass. Children on horses raced across the high meadows. My husband was a college professor; I was a city-bred wife. Could this ever be our family?

In their youth, like so many other pilgrim artists, my Jewish parents had left Hungary for the culture of exile in Paris. At the apex of the Great Depression, in 1937, before Hitler and his collaborators claimed all of Europe, they fled Paris and settled for good in the United States. That's why I grew up without the possibility of knowing my great-aunts or second cousins, for those who stuck to the homeland had gone to the ovens of Auschwitz. Mobility was the lesson. Don't tie yourself to one place. Montparnasse is where I was born; Chicago the dwelling of childhood; and after I married David at nineteen, Seattle is where we lived and had babies and studied until he was offered an instructor's job at the University of Montana.

In 1964, when David and I came to Montana with our first-born two boys, friends in Seattle made bets about how long we would stay. They were not betting against Dave. He had grown up in a small Minnesota town and liked to fish and hunt and keep to himself. But me? I went to concerts and art shows and walked in Chinatown. I shopped for teas, rice wine, and spices whose names I could not pronounce. Home was streets full of strangers, green leafy vegetables thrown away into the rain-filled gutters. The chickens for sale in fly-blown markets were alive and squawking.

"Montana?" said one friend. "I give you a year. Maybe two." Two, because she knew how stubborn I can be. In our private mythology I was the grasshopper, and everyone knows a grasshopper will never turn into an ant.

A quarter century later David is dead, three of our four boys are gone from Missoula, and I'm still living outback in Montana. I am that woman chopping her wood.

The first day—the day I first saw our home place—a sign at the cattle guard read "County road maintenance ends here." I have added my own sign in day-glow scarlet letters, "No hunting or trespassing." Sometimes

I lock the gate so no one can drive onto the quarter mile of dirt road that leads to my house. It's not that I despise people, I simply love to weed my garden in solitude. Sometimes I think I am attached to my piece of ground like a spirit, like the ghosts of its immigrant settlers. Sometimes I feel rooted as the western larch and ponderosa pine. I think everything that has ever lived here inhabits the place, even the migrating birds: kestrels, snipe, bluebirds, red-tail hawks. I think the place inhabits me.

Elk on new grass in May are part of the life I have chosen, and a yellow brittle day in late August when a honey-colored bear cub lies belly-up in a thornapple thicket heedlessly stripping ripe berries as I pull knapweed from the roadside, maybe thirty yards upwind. A coyote bitch and two pups den in the culvert under the road. From our log house on the meadow, I study the coyotes through binoculars. No two days are the same, no season returns, and I am never bored with the stories I find in this land. I live in my city.

There is a recurring vision of a house I have dreamed since I was a girl, so vivid I thought for years it was an actual place. Until one morning I recognized it as dream.

The house in my dream is Victorian, with gabled roofs and a tower. The roof is tiled in red clay, warm and Spanish, substantial and abstract as a Cezanne. Sometimes the roof is blue. Always there are chimneys. Many chimneys.

The upper stories are sided in white-painted cedar shingles, weathered to where the wood shows through. The house sits on high ground. I cannot remember ever finding it hidden in a valley. It has stood for generations surrounded by gardens of poppies, blue cornflowers, flashing white daisies and climbing roses. There is a hedge of heavy-scented purple lilac, and the sounds of winged insects. A few tall deciduous trees—oaks or maples, I'm not sure which—shade the house in cool green refracted light.

I often come upon this place on a walk, see it rise out of mist in a soft Northwest Coast rain. I am never there in the night or in snow, although I love winter. Sunset is possible. The house exists in pastoral separateness, not on a farm. Not in the city. There are no animals, except a shepherd dog who sometimes walks by my side. I've had two such dogs.

The entrance and main rooms are built of multi-colored rock glowing amber and aquamarine, like river stones under running water. There are spacious rooms paneled in mahogany, and a maroon velvet window seat where I can curl up and look through leaded windows. The birds are outside and cannot get in—ruby-throated hummingbirds, large and silent as bats. I flinch at the beat of their emerald wings.

Stairways surprise me. I find them where I least expect, always with delight, and explore where they lead. My bedroom is the tower.

There might be people—mother and father, old friends from school, my little-girl sisters, my grandmother speaking Hungarian, a baby son. David, the fair boy I married before either of us had grown up, is usually someplace, with me or in another room. Perhaps I am making this up out of memories rather than dreams. The people are vague. What I remember so clearly is the house.

David and I studied plans for packaged cedar houses. We labored over hand-drawn blueprints for a remodeled hip-roofed barn with a study and bedroom in the hay loft. Our most elaborate fantasy was inspired by a mine shaft near the ghost town of Garnet, three levels stepping down a slope to the creek. We photographed the site from every angle and measured the dimensions. At the top of the shaft we would build an octagonal book-lined gazebo with views all around. Terraced walkways with solar panels and greenhouse orange trees would connect one level to the next. A great plan for millionaires.

We had started our search for land to build on in the Bitterroot, the paradise valley of western Montana where the Flathead Indians had lived amid such abundance: deer, elk, ducks and geese, cutthroat trout, lush berries and camas and pink bitterroot in spring. We almost bought fourteen acres of swamp on the Bitterroot River at the mouth of Lolo Creek, where Lewis and Clark had made their camp. They named it Traveler's Rest.

> (Lewis) July 3, 1806. *The mosquitoes were so excessively troublesome this evening that we were obliged to kindle large*

*fires for our horses. These insects torture them in such
manner until they placed themselves in the smoke of the fires,
that I really thought they would become frantic.*

Mosquitoes were not in our plans. Neither were swamps, no matter how filled with history. We were looking for open land on a river loaded with native trout, or a stream, or a lake. It had to be within half an hour of the University in Missoula, where David taught courses in Victorian literature and the Romantic poets. Finding nothing suitable in the Bitterroot, we expanded our search to the Clark Fork valley from Clinton to Alberton, and up toward the Flathead as far as Evaro Hill.

David wanted space and silence. "I want to be backed up against wilderness," he said. "No neighbors I can see. Nothing."

He had his reasons. Dave was thirty-seven and I was thirty-four, and already life seemed to be closing down on us. An athlete since childhood, a high-school star who went to college on a basketball ride, David couldn't walk fast without losing his breath. He was afraid to pick up our chubby three-year-old twins.

For two years we had known David was suffering an incurable metabolic disorder. Cholesterol his body could not process clogged his coronary arteries nearly to closure. Twice he had been rushed to the intensive-care ward of St. Patrick's Hospital, and we had recently returned from the University of Washington medical center, one of the best in the country. Specialists had ruled out a bypass operation. "It's not advisable in your case." In fact, the damage was too far gone; we were left with no medical hope. Researchers had not yet developed the miniscule balloons you can insert into clogged veins to clear them out, or laser surgery to burn away the fatty deposits. David was suffering a disease of the heart that we knew would lead inevitably to premature dying.

Death was coming, but we did not know where or when, and we looked for solace in nature undisturbed. With our four boys we hoped to escape into space and silence and privacy. We would go away into the illusion that time could not touch us.

"I want to listen to the moon rise." David yearned for the comfort of old slow cycles. Indian moons and harvests and minute changes of a season as it turns.

Our realtor, having exhausted all prospects in three valleys, offered his hole card. "There's twenty acres on a year-around stream called Bear Creek," he said. "Some of the best trout fishing you'll ever see. You boys like to hunt?" The two older boys, Eric who was fourteen and Steve, twelve, nodded although they had never hunted anything larger than a duck. "White-tails and elk," the realtor said. "I'm telling you the hunting's out of sight."

This particular Bear Creek (there are hundreds of them in Montana) flows into the Blackfoot River some twenty miles northeast from Missoula. It is snow-belt country, high and cold, and you must travel to it on Highway 200, a narrow, icy asphalt ribbon that winds through the canyon of the Blackfoot until the land opens from lichen-encrusted cliffs to what is called Camas Prairie. Bad roads and worse weather protect this area from the commuter subdivisions of the mild Bitterroot. In the fall of 1970 good land was still available, still cheap.

The realtor turned right on Bear Creek Road, over the culvert where Union Creek widens to form a small pond. In years to come, I would study muskrats in that pond.

We would be bundled in some four-wheel-drive vehicle—a Land Rover, a Blazer, a Subaru—waiting for the 7:30 A.M. school bus to take our youngest boys five miles up the road to the three-room school at Potomac, or the older ones twenty miles to the high school in Missoula. As dawn lighted far-off peaks of the Bob Marshall Wilderness to the east, the black pond turned silver, and then salmon pink. The boys and I watched a resident beaver for a couple of months, until he disappeared; a black bear sow bathed with her cubs.

When it was David's turn to drive the kids to the highway, he took a favorite book, like Kipling's *Just-So Stories*, and read aloud "The Cat Who Walks By Itself." The heater hummed in the Land Rover, he breathed the stink of little-boy bodies, and the windows were coated with steam.

East toward the wide and fertile Blackfoot Valley were fields of oats and alfalfa, scattered pastures, cattle, a few houses, and double-wides where loggers and truckers lived. Three miles and two cattle guards up the gravel track curling through a pine forest, we turned at Bear Creek Ranch.

Jack pines abruptly opened to rolling highland meadows burnt by early frosts, dotted with scarlet-leaved bushes. I would come to know the special flavors and culinary uses of each species: the blue mealy service-berry is fine to pick and nibble as you walk; thornapple is best for the birds and bears; and chokecherry makes a pungent wine-red jam and syrup for your pancakes. Timbered hills rose to the south and west, clearcuts pocketing the ridges, and beyond them stood unassuming Mt. Olson dusted with September snow. I got out of the rig to open the gate.

"Forest Service?" I asked, eyeing the scarred forest. "Anaconda, mostly," said the realtor. "From here to Bonner and over the top to Clinton. Like you wanted, this is the end of the public road."

I hated those clearcuts, but the woods around them were dark with tall pine and streaked with western larch beginning their turn to brilliant yellow. The meadows tipped downward, emptying due north into the Big Blackfoot River. Across the river at the northern horizon, hills rose above Gold Creek to the distant Rattlesnake Mountains.

Before driving any farther, we stopped to regard the view. Ranch buildings clustered on the western slope of the adjoining property, etched in flat autumn light. The old homestead was dominated by a great log barn with a high-pitched silvery shake roof and a wide-mouthed loft. Next to the barn was an outsized cement-block garage, a tall narrow grainery, a pig-pen, and a shed. The long and low hewn-log ranch house stood across from the barn, and beyond it were a log bunkhouse, a henhouse, a small cabin, and a newish red-painted frame structure. Except for the barn, all the buildings were roofed in tin, shining like mirrors in the bright afternoon.

A couple dozen white-face Herefords grazed with their heavy calves among huge rock piles in the surrounding meadows.

"Will you look at those rocks," said the realtor. "Some poor sonofabitch picked every damned one by hand."

The rock piles were monuments, all right, to the hard-handed Swedes who homesteaded the place in 1882. Christborgs and Petersens cleared the land with cross-cut saws, pulled stumps with teams of work-horses, and built the log house and the barn. They pried rocks from the heavy clay soil and hauled them to the piles on stoneboats, so they could till the fields for barley and oats.

After World War I, the Swedes sold out to a clan of Yugoslavs. The new immigrants completed an elaborate gravity-flow irrigation system with ditches and a wooden flume that channeled water from Bear Creek over two miles of shale mountainsides to empty at the top of the meadow. They fenced and watered the hundred acres of cleared land into a perfection of farming that made this homestead a show piece. Yankee ranchers from the valley would come to marvel at its green grainfields when their own bottomland pastures were stunted and starved.

All this I discovered in time, starting with the history embedded in the title to the land. But that first day I felt caught with wonder, a sense of recognition from a part of my being I did not know. Here, so unexpected, was home. Not the Victorian house of my dreams, but a homestead I could live on. It belonged to someone else. I never thought it could be ours.

The twenty acres of creek land the realtor had brought me to see was impossible. Too narrow, too damp, too dark in the depths of Bear Creek canyon, weedy. I made the realtor stop again at the top of the hill. "This," I said, pointing to the homestead ranch. Could he find us such a place? And what would it cost?

"Wait just a minute," he said. I could almost see his mind flip through a catalog of Polaroids: dim, boxy houses with daylight basements; modern ranchettes and prefab barns; treeless subdivision lots—one artless image after another. The realtor frowned. "I think that place there, that one hundred sixty, the Vannoy place. It might be for sale."

And it was. One hundred and sixty-three acres. A section of land is 640 acres; a quarter-section is 160 acres; we got an extra three to adjust for the curvature of the earth. It's a good uneven number. Nature will not conform to right angles or triangles or circles marked with a surveyor's transit. Adjusted to the curvature of the earth was just fine. For $56,000 the whole shebang could be ours.

Subsistence homesteading has never been easy in Montana. After World War II it became a loser's game. Since 1948, when they bought the place from the Yugoslavs, the Vannoys had struggled to make a living off a starvation outfit. They raised eight children in the one-and-a-half-story ranch house. Clara and the kids tended the stock and the hay and the garden, while Walter tried to keep the large family solvent by hiring out as a gyppo logger and hauling cattle in his truck and trailer livestock rig.

I often wonder what the Vannoys thought of us when we knocked on their door, eager to buy their land. It was the era of the *Whole Earth Catalog,* and log houses had become fashionable among intellectuals searching for authenticity. True country people saw them as crude and uncivilized. If you could afford the materials, you would cover your logs with aluminum siding.

The Vannoys had covered their walls with sheetrock, which offered insulation, and respectability. The worn plank floors were hidden under linoleum in the kitchen, blue shag carpeting in the living room. The low-eaved upper story served as a dormitory bedroom for children. We knew at once we would tear off the sheetrock.

With most of their children grown and gone off, the Vannoys wanted out. They had pasture for their cattle and horses on the Clearwater, twenty miles upriver, and wanted to lease a nearby truck-stop restaurant. Walter and Clara dreamed of trading backwoods isolation for roadside commerce, just what we were trying to escape. Our downpayment would help build them a new modern house, and the monthly payments would be a twenty-year insurance against failure. We closed the deal in December of 1970—the best Christmas present, ever—and began the work of building a hideout.

Fear had transfixed David in melancholia ever since he discovered his heart disease three years earlier. The rest of us lived under his cloud. As we prepared to move to our new home, his depression seemed to be lifting. Each day of manual labor on the ranch gave David the strength he longed for, and feared. He knew overexertion could bring on a fatal attack.

But David put worry out the window. He stopped calling his cardiologist at each new twinge of angina, laid off on his blood-thinning medicines, and filled his mind with plans for improving things. Our strategy for survival was working. Each weekend, and whenever else we could manage, David and I and our carpenter/writer friend, Jon Jackson, arrived at the homestead with tools and lumber. We were transforming the red-painted shack built to shelter Christmas-tree harvesters into a study. We wanted a quiet, private room to work in, a library for our books.

On the last Sunday of January a Chinook rainstorm pelted down on three feet of snow, and the Blackfoot country became a sheet of glare ice with snow-melt rivers running over it. David and Jon and I, along with the older boys, Eric and Steve, and the three-year-old twins, Andrew and Alex, got stuck without chains on the steepest grade of Bear Creek Road. We carried our tools the last quarter-mile to the ranch.

Walter and Clara were pulling out in their pickup as we arrived. We sloshed past the ranch house to the red shack and went to work painting our new bookshelves that rose from floor to ceiling. When dusk came, we trooped downhill to visit our neighbors on the creek, and they warmed us with hot chocolate, gave us a ride in their chained-up Toyota 4×4, and pulled our car out of the ditch. Gliding back to Missoula over black ice, even the kids were silent, content with the direction our lives were taking.

I will never forget the phone call that awakened me before sunrise the next morning, Monday, January 30, 1971.

"Hello, Annick? This is Walter."

"Walter who?" I asked, trying to shake some waking dream.

"This is Walter, and I'm afraid I've got bad news." It was too early for bad news.

Walter's next words came in loud and clear. "The house burned down. We come to feed the cows this morning, and there was nothing left but the ashes."

As all of us slept, the storm had whirled and gusted with lightning, thunder, and driving rain, and somehow the fire the Vannoys had left burning low in the barrel stove in the ranch house got out of control.

"Or maybe it was the wiring," said Walter.

No one saw the house burn down, except for the cows in their stalls, who must have shrunk back from the blazing light.

I drove to see the ruins with the insurance adjuster. Damage control was my domain. Walter was right. Not a log remained.

The out-of-focus Polaroids the adjuster took as evidence of loss showed a cement-lined hole that had been the root cellar; and the brick chimney red against the melting snow and smoking ash; and me in a yellow slicker looking down at the mess. I carried one of those photos in my wallet for years, until I lost the wallet. It was my *memento mori*—a reminder of what? Fate? It seemed nothing would ever work right for us again.

Barn swallows cry in alarm and circle as their meticulously crafted mud-dauber nests fall from a high eave to shatter on the ground. I wonder if they grieve. How quickly they quit crying and rebuild. I am tempted to see purpose in their actions, a will like my own. Or are they simply puppets to a genetically coded program? Either way, I doubt if you could stop them.

Humans are not much different. After the old house burned down, we used our $12,000 insurance money to put up a new one in the midst of the meadow. We didn't build it from scratch; our house is recycled. David and I found it while trout fishing where the Big Blackfoot joins the

North Fork south of Ovando. Massive even at a distance, the abandoned log house sat on a broad field of sagebrush and wild iris like a mirage of the good life. The walls were made of hewn logs a foot and a half wide and twenty-six feet long. They had been squared with a broad axe and adze, fitted together with dovetail joints. With two full stories, a steeply pitched gabled roof, and a lean-to kitchen, the structure was designed like a Midwestern farmhouse, not a log cabin. We were the only people who wanted it.

We bought the house for $200 from an absentee landlord, a dentist in Moses Lake. David and I camped there all of June, living in a sky-blue six-person wall tent with our four boys, a Siamese cat, a German Shepherd, and a black Lab puppy named Shy Moon. Jon came to help us out. By the campfire one cool star-lit evening, he taught the older boys to chug Jim Beam. The next morning they were pale and wobbly, but hard at work, initiated into the rites of mountain manhood.

Together, we tore the old house down. With malletts and crowbars, Jon and Eric and Steve smashed the plastered walls and dismembered the roof beams. Dave and I pulled nails, carefully saved the weathered hand-milled siding to use again as interior paneling. Then we stamped a number into each log, matching the numbers to diagrams Dave drew. The house would be rebuilt like a giant's lincoln-log puzzle on our homestead thirty miles downriver.

That June was a blessed season, all of us living out-of-doors, the twins barefoot and sunburnt. We fished in the Blackfoot for breakfast trout, and bathed in it after work. At sunset we got out baseball mitts and bats and a ball and played pickup softball on the sagebrush flat.

Friends came on the Fourth of July weekend to help stack the heavy hand-hewn logs onto the Vannoy's logging truck. We hauled the whole house and a barn and a blacksmith's shed back to Bear Creek in three loads. After the fireworks, we celebrated with a picnic of hot dogs, potato salad, watermelon, and beer.

Like the Swedes who homesteaded our piece of ground, and the unknown pioneers on the Blackfoot who had created an American Gothic farmhouse out of virgin timbers, we were going to build our own home on our own land.

"Watch out," I have warned friends who speak lightly of building a house. "If you build it, be sure you want it. The place will own you." We settled the huge timbers carefully into place, fitting each into perfect dovetail joints, and even death could not turn me loose.

David died in May of 1974. It was a warm wildflower day, and he had been irrigating our hay meadow. I was in the new house cooking stew for dinner. The twins were playing with toy soldiers on the maple floor we had salvaged from the Hellgate High School gym, and the older boys had gone off to the Aber Day kegger concert on Miller Creek. David was washing up at the kitchen sink.

"Oh dear," he said, turning to me with a quizzical look. David just fell down and died. There was no way I could bring him back.

Snow fell the next morning, and I awoke from my first night of grief to find six elk grazing on new meadow grass, pawing the wet snow under my living-room window. Know that this is true. My boys are grown and mostly gone. I live on my homestead alone some nights, and some nights with a man I love and cherish. I have a calico cat and a young shepherd dog, and four horses I rarely ride.

From the wide kitchen windows we built ourselves, I love to watch my horses as they top the high ridge of the meadow and graze their way down toward the house. Most of the seven windows are cracked. The fir frames were too green when we put in the double-insulated panes of glass, and one hot August day four windows cracked one after the other from the uneven pressures of drying wood. The sounds they made were like shots from a rifle.

We cut and stack hay each summer, and I toss bales from the loft of the log barn to feed the horses each winter. Almaree is the lame old quarterhorse mare; Eustacia, her foal, was born in an April blizzard the month we moved onto our land; the wild-eyed gelding, Hermano, was Stephen's birthday present when he turned thirteen; and Buck is a visitor left by a bronc-riding poet friend. They are going to fat, and wild, but those horses have come to own the land as much as I do.

A couple of years after Dave died, I dreamed my Victorian house again. It was a warm night in July, too hot for blankets. The kids were gone to visit my parents in their summer home on Lake Michigan, and I was alone, feeling abandoned in the high empty bedroom with its skylight above the double bed, and tall uncurtained windows looking out to the meadows. The Bear Creek Valley and the pine-forested hills glowed soft muted blue in the moon's light. I tossed a long time in my moonlit bed before falling into sleep.

The house I entered was familiar, but somehow sinister. Its rooms were a rambling maze, and I was lost in their turnings. The lower story was walled with stone, the windows leaded, walls paneled in mahogany, and window seats upholstered in velvet.

I was not content to sit in my usual place and look out at gardens of poppies and roses. I was searching for David. I climbed staircase after staircase, and finally arrived at my bedroom in the tower.

The many-sided room was full of sunlight, and I breathed easier. I heard laughter and wandered to a window. Outside, tall as the house, was an apple tree in full bloom. I opened the window, leaned out to pick white blossoms. But I could not reach the bough.

A man sat in the highest branches. It was David, blue-eyed, blond as he had been when I first knew him, but he was not a boy anymore. I called to him. He did not answer. He smiled, though, and I knew he was happy. He was smiling at me.

I awoke feeling comforted. I heard the odd, creaking talk of swallows building their mud-dauber nests under the peaked eaves of our roof. Early-morning sun slid into open windows. I was home, and not alone. Out by the stone pile a long-eared coyote cried the day alive. We can never be abandoned. The love you have will never abandon you.

THE VIEW FROM MY WINDOW

William Hjortsberg

A friend tells an apocryphal story about a world-renowned poet whose vast reputation afforded a certain unsought celebrity. As a consequence of his fame, the poet became the darling of the social set and soon found himself married to a dynamic dabbler in the arts. Although her friends felt she'd made a marvelous catch, the marriage didn't last a year. Asked about the divorce, the woman sneered: "I thought I was getting a Nobel Prize candidate and ended up with some bum who spends all his time staring out the window."

The story has a special resonance for writers, especially those like me who live lost in daydreams. A window is an operational necessity. If it has a great view, so much the better. Looking back twenty-five years, I remember my various work places with the wistful nostalgia of an aging roué recalling lost lovers. In most ways, it was always the same room. Only the views were different.

There was a twelve-dollar-a-month farmhouse on the Balearic Island of Formentera with no glass in the wood-shuttered windows. The view from the second-story loft reached across a grove of almond trees to the Mediterranean. Another island: St. Croix, one of the Virgins. No Caribbean view here. I lived far up Mahogany Road and worked in an abandoned brooder coop with a corrugated tin roof and walls of chicken wire. The view was in all directions: tamarind and mango trees; sly mongooses slinking between the hibiscus and oleander, mourning doves clinging to the power lines like musical notation on a staff. In Bolinas, California, the back bedroom window above my make-shift desk looked out across a broad pasture to the coast range north of Tamalpias. In Costa Rica, there was a house at Playa Bonita where I stared at the Caribbean for hours at a stretch. It was the curling surf of the Pacific on the coast of Jalisco in Mexico. No windows here. I worked in the mornings at a small seafood stand on the beach at Barra de Navidad. My portable Royal sat on a tin table advertising Carta Blanca beer. The place had no walls, just a palapa overhead and white sand underfoot. I'd quit when the wind came up at noon, threatening to blow my novel-in-progress all the way to Guadalajara. Nature's way of saying it was time to go surfing.

Of all the memorable views, the best have been framed by Montana windows. For ten years I lived in Paradise Valley south of Livingston, in a lovely house built around the turn of the century by a long-forgotten lawyer. He had an office on the third floor, a single-room turret with windows on three sides affording views of the Absarokas. Apparently, lawyers have no use for daydreams. The windows were tiny and the field of vision severely restricted. A tank driver gets a better view from inside an M-60.

After a divorce, self-imposed exile began in a shabby furnished apartment in Livingston. Back in the days of Calamity Jane, the place was the town's contagion hospital. Every time I swept the floor, I had visions of cholera germs rising with the dust out of the cracks. The view was across the smoking rooftops and the railroad yard to where the panoramic Sleeping Giant stretched like T. S. Eliot's "patient etherized upon a table."

Next, I moved briefly to Hawaii which, as a honeymoon spot, surely must share the bill with Oscar Wilde's impression of Niagara Falls: "The second greatest disappointment in every young bride's life." I suppose I had a view. Most of the time torrential rain made it impossible to say what it was. A film project took me to London for a year. Not much improvement in the rain department and so what if the view was half an acre of parking lot at Pinewood Studios . . . this was England, and I was on per diem.

Returning to Montana after a two-year absence, I mailed out a change-of-address card: "Hallelujah!! I've moved back to the mountains." Home was a small log cabin up the Boulder River above McLeod. The ceilings were low, the walls needed rechinking, the well wasn't hooked-up . . . but the view was fantastic! It made you want to shout, "Come back, Shane!"

Four years later, the shout still echoes, even on days like today when a snowstorm screens the saddle of Green Mountain and draws a gray veil over the stern limestone features of the Lion Head. Curtained by clouds, the view exists only in memory and my imagination projects Caribbean snapshots onto the blank screen. This is much easier than imagining what really lies behind the clouds. How do you conjur up awe?

Of course, what is unseen is always much more important than the view at hand. That's why writers love staring out of windows. Attractive scenery fuels the mechanism. Breathtaking vistas provide the highest octane, but there is always the danger of beauty-overload and creative flame-out. Then you just sit and stare, dumbfounded, poleaxed by landscape and sky, another victim of the sunset.

At best, a fabulous view opens a mysterious door into the unknown. I stare at the red-and-ochre façade of the Lion Head looming above the cabin and see nothing of the eponymous feline profile. (I've always had trouble with that. To me, the abrupt cliff looks more like the physiognomy of a gorilla.) What I imagine is the immense wall of glacial ice grinding down from the Beartooth plateau, scooping and shaping the valley where I live, sculpting the Lion Head from the ancient upthrust strata of limestone seabed, scattering like a child's discarded marbles the profusion of smooth granite boulders that give the meandering mountain river its name.

Staring at my incredible view, I think of places tucked out of sight by the contours of landscape. Places I've walked and explored. The natural bridge and dry waterfall in a narrow canyon on the Boulder just across the gravel road. (This is a dubious tourist attraction; quite spectacular when the 110 foot falls are flowing, but somewhat disappointing since a subterranean channel enlarged a couple years back, draining the entire river as if God had pulled the plug.)

An abandoned nineteenth-century logging operation lies hidden under the timber on the crest of Baker Mountain. The long skid still cuts down the steep slope. Thick coiling cable and a rusting cast-iron flywheel thrust abruptly from the forest floor. Gleaming in a fold behind rugged Tepee Mountain and its taller sister, Contact, sits a small lake I've never seen. I know it only from the details of a U.S. Geological Survey map. Some day soon, I plan on hiking up there, fitting another piece in the mysterious puzzle of my magnificent view.

It's the mystery I thrive on. Perhaps that's why I've never been to the unnamed lake, or why in four years' time I've yet to stand on the brow of the Lion Head. The moon is a more romantic place to those not born to be astronauts. In winter, I infrequently see bald eagles cruising over the Boulder River. Occasional sandhill cranes and Canadian geese fly by. The days when I see nothing makes their sudden appearance more wonderful, just as a lovely sound is informed by the silence surrounding it.

The mule deer grazing outside my window are as common as the cottontails hiding under the porch and almost as invisible. Once for the briefest of moments, I caught a cougar in my headlights as he bounded up the driveway. Since then, I've never seen another, although I frequently find their tracks as Baker Draw behind the cabin provides a convenient passage over to the West Boulder. On Christmas morning, fresh pug marks cut across the overnight snowfall on my deck. A crystalline day with silver trees glistening against an empyrean sky, yet those tracks contained my entire field of vision. The big cat pacing my imagination was more real than all the deer grazing on the hillside. And when a chinook blew up and swept the powder away, the tracks remained; saucer-sized circles of ice marking the deck like the footprints of a tangible ghost.

With all this gazing out of windows, the wonder is that I ever get anything done. I seem to work best at night when dark and shadows hide the remarkable view. In those silent hours the landscape of the imagination comes alive. Darkness turns my window into an obscure mirror and, looking up from the keyboard, I confront not scenery but the hollow unwavering stare of my unforgiving reflection.

MORE THAN SKIN DEEP

Glenn Law

I wasn't born in Montana; I don't live there now. But I was born to it and, even now, it is still home.

I first went to Montana as a student, sprung from the Midwestern suburbs, looking for something more, perhaps adventure. Missoula was no disappointment, although later the things I came to regard as essentially Montana would speak to me from east of the Continental Divide.

After my third year of studenting I didn't leave the state when school let out. I took a job in southwestern Montana. This is range and ranch country, broad valleys and arid benchlands. Rivers run north here and so do the mountains. Range after range of snowpeaks stand soldiered against the sky. Vistas are elegant and vast. I came into this country as ranch labor and was given 1,500 sheep to summer on the high meadows of the Gravelly Range.

Herding sheep is an odd job, aside from providing stock material for a lot of regional jokes. The job as it is done in southwestern Montana has scarcely changed over the last century. Pickup trucks have replaced buckboards in camptending chores, but otherwise every day is a replay of any number of summer days twenty-five or fifty or seventy-five years ago.

The theory is simple. Mountain grass packs a protein wallop and fattens lambs quickly. The Forest Service leases grazing allotments cheap. The assignment is: minimize the impact of 1,500 grazers on The People's land and maximize the yield, in pounds of flesh, to The Rancher's pocket.

Working with a couple of horses and a dog, you move the sheep across the rich high pastures, keeping them in new grass and protecting them from the things they can't protect themselves from, which is almost everything, most of all themselves. Your basic sheep is a pretty simple package. Look into a sheep's eyes and you can see the back of its skull. All the qualities that make *Ovis* so splendid a genus in the wild have been mostly bred out of the domestic variety. All that remains of the noble lineage is the instinct to breed and eat—and the phenomenal ability to wander comfortably in the meanest terrain. This last one is a propensity sheep exercise daily.

In the herder's role as protector, it is essential to anticipate where sheep will go, and if it isn't a place you are willing to follow, steer them away from it. They are likely to survive where their feet carry them, but losing sheep out of the band is bad business; and you could get yourself killed trying to scrape them out of some of the places they can get into.

So the job develops as a daily confrontation with the landscape. A rocky canyon, a heavy piece of sidehill timber, any place sheep might amble in a few hours becomes a concern. In the solitude of herding, landscape becomes more than a consideration. It becomes personal space.

If you don't know about personal space, next time you get on a crowded elevator (granted, hard to find in Montana—both the elevator and the crowd) don't turn around after you walk on. The discomfort, yours and the other passengers', will teach you everything you need to know about personal space, between floors.

Personal space is variable. Often it is no bigger than the inside of our car. Its boundaries may be the edge of a desk. It varies from person to person but more importantly it adjusts to the situation at hand. It expands or contracts to include the area surrounding you that can have an immediate effect on your well being and security.

On the high Gravelly personal space becomes immense. Of course it takes in the dog, the horses, and the sheep—but also where they might wander and all the things that can affect them. Light and darkness, sun and rain all play a lively role in every day and become an immediate concern. This critical personal space takes in a sizeable piece of geography.

From the crest of the Gravelly this space reaches east across the Madison to the Hilgards; south past the Park into Idaho, beyond Driggs and the back of the Tetons; over the Centennial into Idaho to the southwest; to the west, beyond the Pioneers; and north across the plains toward Canada. Anything that happens in this space affects how your day is going to go. The storm coming out of Idaho across the Blacktail is a dead ringer to cross the Upper Ruby and hit late in the afternoon, bringing rain and darkness a couple of hours early. That storm is in your space.

There are few places where personal space has the license or the need to unleash itself like this. None are so startlingly beautiful as Montana.

Montana's beauty can be deceptive because it is easy to recognize. It is a familiar quality and quick to grasp. But lots of places are beautiful, yet they lack the special power Montana has. The beauty can haze you into thinking you have the whole story, but it hides something more subtle and beguiling. The sparse population in Montana is also easy to grasp and it complements the beauty of the landscape; but there is something at work here broader than the lack of crowds, something that reaches deeper than the agreeable play of light and shape on the retina.

Montana's special gift is space, landscape made personal; space that reaches out to the horizon then comes back and gets under your skin. It reaches inward, wraps itself around your soul, incubates and grows. When you finally begin to understand just what it is about Montana that is important to you, it has already taken root in your heart and you'll never be the same.

The grip of these spaces is elusive. It doesn't show itself promiscuously. But it is essential to understanding Montana and why it has a hold on you. I learned it through the extreme, but you don't have to chase sheep in the mountains to feel it. Once it has taken root, and it always does, you feel it in towns, in a theater, at work or walking down the sidewalk in Billings. You know it is there, if only at the edge of consciousness, the sweep of landscape, reassuring and vital. Once you feel it, it's always with you, always there.

In Helena late one night I was drawn from the house by an unfamiliar sound, the call of swans overhead. A small band circled the valley. As they passed over, the lights of the city reflected off their breasts and undersides of their wings. They circled out beyond the city lights, calling still, and other smaller bands flew out of the darkness to join them. They circled a long time, gathering numbers, then broke for the south and flew into the darkness. I felt the space then, the space where swans come from in the night and the space they would traverse, both unknown but both important.

Montana spaces can be subtle and confusing, like on the Highline along the Canadian border. Here in the serious wheat and cereal country the landscape wears a familiar face, cultivated fields stretching over rolling hills following one after another. But the scale is all wrong. The gentle rises of the land, from crest to crest, lie eight or ten miles apart. It may take ten minutes of highway driving to get from one rounded top to another. It's disorienting country and it can make you feel small like no other.

Eastern Montana, the high plains, has its own special brand of space.

It's sneaky and it's powerful and it's not for everyone. I lived in Montana for more than a decade before I acquiesced to my fascination with the plains. It started in the Judith Gap country and quickly spread east, south of Ekalaka where it ran the risk of getting mixed up with Dakota and Wyoming. At times it pulled harder than my loyalty to the rivers and ranges of southwestern Montana.

The northern plains give meaning to the words "open" and "desolate." Beauty is not in familiar form. Far more evident is the space itself, and you first have to come to grips with the space before you can begin to see the beauty. For hundreds of miles nothing turns or breaks the wind. The land lies stark and flat under a thin sky that doesn't touch down at the horizon, just disappears in the distance. Barbed wire sings songs here.

Intricacies of landscape, valleys, coulees, and canyons are incised into the plains. You don't see them until you are at their brink. This is a complex landscape, deceiving, mostly hidden and inverted. The space is immense. Landscape features that are the star of the show in other places are not imposing here. They get lost in the space. Distant ranges of mountains stand alone, isolated, and only punctuate the economy of line and vast scale of the plains. This kind of space can make you feel alone on the planet. It too is haunting and pervasive.

The power of spaces in Montana isn't always blatant and grand. The details can be just as consuming.

The rivers of southwestern Montana are some of the world's finest trout streams and fishing is a game dedicated to such details.

On a trout stream only the space near to hand is important. The immediate stretch of river you confront holds enough challenge to eclipse everything beyond its strict boundaries, if just for a little while. The entire world is reduced to a single riffle. As you work that stretch of water, casting and watching, the places that hold trout reveal themselves. A trout shows, feeding on the surface, and the riffle fades into the periphery: the five-foot stretch of moving water above the trout assumes larger proportions. The fly is cast and everything depends on its perfect drift along the precise line of flow that leads to where the trout lies holding in the current. The fly finds its path on the invisible intricacies and variations in the surface film, tiny currents within larger patterns. The critical space further contracts to a few square inches of moving water beneath the fly. These square inches become large as details are revealed. The fly spins, glides onto an unseen stillness in the current, hesitates, dancing on hackle tips over a break in the flow in a slow precision. Concentration of space begets an expanded timesense. The fluid events of a second or two unfold distinctly, slowly. Beneath the surface, movement begins and the trout separates itself from the riverbottom and begins rising through the flow to intercept the fly. The fish tips up, mouth closes around the fly, and he heads back down. The miniature world gives way, details vanish, replaced by the riffle once again where the contest will be played and you answer the pull of wild life against a fine strand of nylon and a light wire hook.

Contest ended, the tension can't hold. You sit back on the bank and the space opens up around you, across the broad valley, onto the peaks and ridges that trace the horizon like an erratic month on the stock market or a mixed day of angling luck. If it has been an ordinary day of fishing, with problems and solutions, failures and successes, you can see your day graphed along the crest of the mountains, peaks and valleys along the ridge leading all the way around and coming back to start over through 360° of sky.

Space becomes personal in Montana, a possession, something held in the heart like a favorite view or remembered scene. There's enough space in the state, and few enough people; everyone might well have a favorite view all to themselves and never have to share it with another. The urgency of space is something that is shared, yet remains intensely personal. It's an intimate link with the landscape you carry with you when you live in Montana, or live away from it. It becomes a possession and like any possession that is precious and valuable, it is carefully guarded.

Possessiveness is a trait of the people who live in Montana. They are territorial and protective about their state, emotions usually associated with patriotism and nationalism. This is a quality not evident in many places. People from New Jersey act the same way but the similarity ends there. They seem to be overcompensating for having gotten short shrift on the Hit Parade of States. I suspect Alaskans are as possessive, but I haven't been there to find out.

Loyalty to country and possessiveness is something that newcomers to Montana take to quickly and enthusiastically, in a predictable manner. Just as converts make the most devout Catholics, so newcomers make the most rabidly possessive Montanans. Everyone who moves to Montana wants to be the last one allowed in. They want the immigration gate locked behind them.

Newcomers have always been a part of the state. Flatlander and pilgrim are terms rich with heritage in the state vocabulary. First they came to trap beaver, then graze cattle and sheep. They mined the minerals and later tried to farm with methods sadly suited to Montana's thin soils.

They continue to come, many because the spaces have a hold on them. Some come to buy up vast tracts and subdivide. Slicksmart landtraders, veterans of the real estate circuits in California, Texas, and Florida move into the state and, intoxicated by space, fester for a deal. They lock up their own profits, fence off their own portion of the space, unaware that they destroy what they seek to possess. *No Trespassing* signs blossom overnight along miles of decades-old fenceline. Private property, always sacrosanct here, takes on a new dimension as exclusivity more and more blocks the common claim to land and spaces.

The zealotry of the newcomer, the unbridled ambition to stake a private claim on the spaces, is familiar to native Montanans. They've seen it for years, just as they've seen other kinds of change. Land gets bought and sold. People come and some of them stay. Others just leave scars. They've seen family ranches lost on a bad deal of the cards, sold against low cattle prices, blown away in dry times or just plain drunk up. Change is not without some benefits though, and you take the good along with the bad. Natives are not militant protectionists as a rule. But they do maintain a keen and cynical awareness of who is native and who is not. Newcomers are accepted as part of the flow of years. Still there is always a gap between those born in Montana and those arrived from elsewhere.

To become a legal Montana resident you have to live in the state for a specified period of time and pay state income taxes. But nativity has nothing to do with residency. It's measured in generations, not months or years. The fact will always remain that you have come from somewhere else and no amount of time, no number of winters, can ever really over-come that.

My time in Montana was tied to the mountains and rivers, the land and the water, the spaces and places that are essentially Montana and I remain furiously addicted to the frame of mind that Montana allows. I saw things there and learned things that few others ever do. And like others I know where some things are that I doubt have been seen before or since. I developed the intense regard for space that comes to me more as an awareness than a thought when I think about Montana. I have grown comfortable knowing I'll always have come from somewhere else, even though Montana is my home.

From a long ways away, knowing the space is there is comforting and reassuring. I carry my own precious links to Montana with me and I am protective of my claims to that space.

My son was born in Bozeman and just as I can never be a native he can never be anything but. I hold this claim close. My great-great aunt owned a hotel in Laurel, a railroad town, and the hotel sheltered tran-sient brakemen, conductors, and engineers. I never knew this distant aunt, but the hotel is still there and still bears her name. This bit of lineage, however tenuous, gives me satisfaction in a place where authen-ticity can neither be earned nor bought.

This authenticity is something inviolable in Montana. The most suc-cessful businessman and entrepeneur, the insightful artist, the creative scientist not born here is destined to remain an outsider, no matter how significant their contribution. The most dismally poor career irrigator struggling along on Social Security, teeth gone bad from too many years of Copenhagen, remains a more natural and authentic part of the social landscape by sheer virtue of nativity.

He certainly speaks better for the things you can expect the state to provide for you.

In Montana you have to make your own luck. Milk and honey for the mind don't nourish the body. You can't eat the scenery. There are only so many ways to make a living here and few of them result in material wealth. You can't expect much from a country that plays its hand close and never really shows all its cards. But when it has a hold on you, you find a way to get what you need.

Because the climate is harsh, the geography unforgiving, and the economy often Spartan, it's natural to assume that living in Montana is hard.

"You gotta be tough to live in Montana."

You hear it time and time again. But the quality of life in Montana is high and has nothing to do with the standard of living. Just as the thin soil resists domestication, so the space is comfortable and fertile for the spirit.

The economy has a way of driving out the less committed. The climate takes its toll on the less captivated. But you don't have to be tough to live where the air is clean, water pure, and it will be a cold day in hell before a nuclear reactor moves in next door. It is comfortable living where your spirit and space can reach to the horizon or linger along a trout stream. Living in Montana is easy.

Leaving it is hard.

STRAWBERRIES UNDER ICE

David Quammen

1

The Gradient of Net Mass Balance

The center of Greenland lies eleven hundred feet below sea level, giving the great frozen island somewhat the profile of an atoll. The reason for that sunken shape is not chiefly geologic; it's not a matter of tectonic vectors, mountain-building lateral pressures, ramming and grinding slabs of earthen crust. The reason is climate. Greenland is squashed to concavity by the weight of its overlying ice. Antarctica is squashed likewise.

Melt the ice away and Greenland's interior would bounce upward, like a pounded-out dent in the roof of a Chevy. Melt the ice (all seven million cubic miles of it) off Antarctica and the Earth itself would change shape. It would become almost spherical. Thaw the state of Montana back to bedrock and who can say what would happen. The damage would be slightly more subtle.

Ice is lighter than water but still heavy. The stuff answers gravity. Ice is a solid but not an absolute solid. The stuff flows. Slowly but inexorably—at one ten-thousandth the rate of springwater under similar conditions of gravity and slope—it runs downhill. We think of iciness as a synonym for cold, but cold is relative and ice happens to function well as insulation against heat loss: low thermal conductivity. Also it *releases* heat to immediate surroundings in the final stage of becoming frozen itself. Ice warms. On the particular night we will come to presently, it warmed me. What it is, ice, is water transmogrified to the crystalline and paradoxical state.

When a tongue of ice flows down a mountain valley we call it a glacier. When it flows out in all directions from a source point at high elevation, like pancake batter poured on griddle, we call it a sheet. Much of Antarctica is covered by a vast single sheet, within which the flow pattern is generally centrifugal but complex, with localized streams and eddies of ice moving independently at different rates. Out at the Antarctic circumference are glaciers and seaborne shelves, from which icebergs calve off under their own weight. On Greenland the arrangement is similar. But this is not an essay about Antarctica and Greenland. Both sheets and glaciers are supplied with their substance, their impetus, their ice, by snow and other forms of precipitation back uphill at the source. Since ice has that certain stiffness, that coy but yielding relationship with gravity, a big heavy glacier runs downhill more quickly than a little light one; a thick high-domed sheet flows outward more quickly than a thin one. While old ice is continually lost by calving and melting in the lowlands, new ice is deposited in the highlands, and any glacier or sheet receiving more new ice than it loses old, through the course of a year, is a glacier or sheet that is growing. The scientists would say that its net mass balance is positive.

The Antarctic sheet has a positive balance. Accumulation of new ice runs ahead of ablation, as the scientists would put it, by some hundred cubic miles yearly. Greenland is a much smaller world of ice with a much smaller balance; the scientists don't even agree whether that balance is just above zero or just below. Greenland may be getting either more icy or less. We live in a warmish interlude to an epoch of great freeze-overs, possibly near the end of that interlude, and by some judgments the total amount of ice on our planet is increasing. On the other hand sea levels are rising, which seems to imply a global decrease in ice; and there's the dire boring problem of human impact on temperatures, from all our stoking of the engines of civilization. Do we stand on the threshold of a new Ice Age or a greenhouse? No one knows. But in the short run Montana at least seems to be getting warmer, God help it.

Each point on a great ice body has its own numerical value for mass balance. Is the ice right here thicker or thinner than last year? Measured at any particular point, is the glacier becoming more robust or less? Is it thriving or dying? The collective profile of all those individual soundings—more ice or less? thriving or dying?—is called the gradient of net mass balance. This gradient tells, in broad perspective, what has been lost and what has been gained. On the night in question, I happened to be asking myself exactly the same: What's been lost and what gained? Because snow gathers most heavily in frigid sky-scraping highlands, the gradient of net mass balance correlates steeply with altitude. Robust glaciers come snaking down out of the Alaskan mountains. Places like central Greenland and Antarctica, squashed low by the weight of ice, have grown their own lofty highlands from ice itself: The bedrock of East Antarctica lies roughly at sea level but the ice surface rises to 13,000 feet. Also because snow gathers most heavily in frigid sky-scraping highlands, I had taken myself on the afternoon preceding the night in question to a drifted-over pass in the Bitterroot Mountains, all hell-and-gone up on the state border just west of the town of Tarkio, Montana, and started skiing uphill from there.

I needed as much snow as possible. I carried food and a goose-down bag and a small shovel. The night in question was December 31, 1975.

I hadn't come to measure depths or calculate gradients. I had come to insert myself into a cold white hole. First, of course, I had to dig it. This elaborately uncomfortable enterprise seems to have been part of a long foggy process of escape and purgation, much of which you can be spared. Suffice that my snow cave, to be dug on New Year's Eve into a ten-foot-high cornice on the leeward side of the highest ridge I could ski to, and barely large enough for one person, would be at the aphelion of that long foggy process. At the perihelion was Oxford University.

At Oxford University during one week in late springtime there is a festival of crew races on the river and girls in long dresses and boys in straw hats and champagne and strawberries. This event is called Eights Week, for the fact of eight men to a crew. It is innocent. More precisely: it is no more obnoxious, no more steeped in snobbery and dandified xenophobia and intellectual and social complacence, than any other aspect of Oxford University. The strawberries are served under heavy cream. Sybaritism is mandatory. For these and other reasons, partly personal, partly political, I had fled the place screaming during Eights Week of 1972, almost precisely coincident (by no coincidence) with Richard Nixon's announcement of the blockade of Haiphong harbor. Nixon's blockade and Oxford's strawberries had nothing logically in common, but they converged to produce in me a drastic reaction to what until then had been just a festering distemper.

It took me another year to arrive in Montana. I had never before set foot in the state. I knew no one there. But I had heard that it was a place where, in the early weeks of September, a person could look up to a looming horizon and see fresh-laid snow. I had noted certain blue lines on a highway map, knew the lines to be rivers, and imagined those rivers to be dark mountain streams flashing with trout. I arrived during the early weeks of September and lo it was all true.

I took a room in an old-fashioned boarding house. I looked for a job. I started work on a recklessly ambitious and doomed novel. I sensed rather soon that I hadn't come to this place temporarily. I began reading the writers—Herodotus, Euripides, Coleridge, Descartes, Rousseau, Thoreau, Raymond Chandler—for whom a conscientious and narrow academic career had left no time. I spent my nest-egg and then sold my Volkswagen bus for another. I learned the clownish mortification of addressing strangers with: "Hi, my name is Invisible and I'll be your waiter tonight." I was twenty-six, just old enough to realize that this period was not some sort of prelude to my life but the thing itself. I knew I was spending real currency, hard and finite, on a speculative venture at an unknowable rate of return: the currency of time, energy, stamina. Two more years passed before I arrived, sweaty and chilled, at that high cold cornice in the Bitterroots.

By then I had made a small handful of precious friends in this new place, and a menagerie of acquaintances, and I had learned also to say: "You want that on the rocks or up?" Time was still plentiful but stamina was low. Around Christmas that year, two of the precious friends announced a New Year's Eve party. Tempting, yet it seemed somehow a better idea to spend the occasion alone in a snow cave.

So here I was. There had been no trail up the face of the ridge and lifting my skis through the heavy snow had drenched and exhausted me. My thighs felt as though the Chicago police had worked on them with truncheons. I dug my hole. That done, I changed out of the soaked freezing clothes. I boiled and ate some noodles, drank some cocoa; if I had been smart enough to encumber my pack with a bottle of wine, I don't remember it. When dark came I felt the nervous exhilaration of utter solitude and, behind that like a metallic aftertaste, loneliness. I gnawed on my thoughts for an hour or two, then retired. The night turned into a clear one and when I crawled out of the cave at three A.M. of the new year, to empty my bladder, I found the sky rolled out in a stunning pageant of scope and dispassion and cold grace.

It was too good to waste. I went back into the cave for my glasses.

The temperature by now had gone into the teens below zero. I stood there beside the cornice in cotton sweatpants, gaping up. "We never know what we have lost, or what we have found," says America's wisest poet, Penn Warren, in the context of a meditation about John James Audubon and the transforming power of landscape. We never know what we have lost, or what we have found. All I did know was that the highway maps called it Montana, and that I was here, and that in the course of a life a person could travel widely but could truly open his veins and his soul to just a limited number of places.

After half an hour I crawled back into the cave, where ten feet of snow and a rime of ice would keep me warm.

2

Ablation

Trace any glacier or ice sheet downhill from its source and eventually you will come to a boundary where the mass balance of ice is zero. Nothing is lost, over the course of time, and nothing is gained. The ice itself constantly flows past this boundary, molecule by molecule, but if any new ice is added here by precipitation, if any old ice is taken away by melting, those additions and subtractions cancel each other exactly. This boundary is called the equilibrium line. Like other forms of equilibrium, it entails a certain cold imperturbability, a sublime stasis relative to what's going on all around. Above the equilibrium line is the zone of accumulation. Below is the zone of ablation.

Ablation is the scientists' fancy word for loss. Down here the mass balance is negative. Ice is supplied to this zone mainly by flow from above, little or not at all by direct precipitation, and whatever does come as direct precipitation is less than the amount annually lost. The loss results from several different processes: wind erosion, surface melting, evaporation (ice does evaporate), underside melting of an ice shelf where it rests on the warmer seawater. Calving off of icebergs. Calving is the scientists' quaint word for that event when a great hunk of ice—as big as a house or, in some cases, as big as a county—tears away from the leading edge of the sheet or the glacier and falls thunderously into the sea.

Possibly this talk about calving reflects an unspoken sense that the larger ice mass, moving, pulsing, constantly changing its shape, is almost alive. If so the analogy doesn't go far. Icebergs don't suckle or grow. They float away on the sea, melt, break apart, disappear. Wind erosion and evaporation and most of those other ablative processes work on the ice slowly, incrementally. Calving on the other hand is abrupt. A large piece of the whole is there, and then gone.

The occurrence of a calving event depends on a number of factors—flow rate of the whole ice body, thickness at the edge, temperature, fissures in the ice, stresses from gravity or tides—one of which is the strength of the ice itself. That factor, strength, is hard to measure. You might never know until too late. Certain experiments done on strength-testing machines have yielded certain numbers: a strength of thirty-eight bars (a bar is a unit of pressure equal to 100,000 newtons per square meter) for crushing; fourteen bars for bending; nine bars for tensile. But those numbers offer no absolute guide to the performance of different types of ice under different conditions. They only suggest in a relative way that, though ice may flow majestically under its own weight, though it may stretch like caramel, though it may bend like lead, it gives back rocklike resistance to a force coming down on it suddenly. None of this cold information was available to me on the day now in mind, and if it had been I wouldn't have wanted it.

On the day now in mind I had been off skiing, again, with no thought for the physical properties of ice, other than maybe some vague awareness of the knee strain involved in carving a turn across boilerplate. I came home to find a note in my door.

The note said that a young woman I knew, the great love of a friend of mine, was dead. The note didn't say what had happened. I should call a number in Helena for details. It was not only shocking but ominous. Because I knew that the young woman had lately been working through some uneasy and confusing times, I thought of all the various grim possibilities involving despair. Then I called the Helena number, where a houseful of friends were gathered for communal grieving and food and loud music. I learned that the young woman had died from a fall. A freak accident. In the coldest sense of cold consolation, there was in this information some relief.

She had slipped on a patch of sidewalk ice, the night before, and hit her head. A nasty blow, a moment or two of unconsciousness, but she had apparently been all right. She went home alone and was not all right and died before morning. I suppose she was about twenty-seven. This is exactly why head-trauma cases are normally put under close overnight observation, but I wasn't aware of that at the time, and neither evidently were the folks who had helped her up off that icy sidewalk. She had seemed okay. Even after the fall, her death was preventable. Of course most of us will die preventable deaths; hers was only more vividly so, and earlier.

I had known her, not well, through her sweetheart and the network of friends now assembled in that house in Helena. These friends of hers and mine were mostly a group of ecologists who had worked together, during graduate school, as waiters and bartenders and cooks; I met them in that context and they had nurtured my sanity to no small degree when that context began straining it. They read books, they talked about ideas, they knew a spruce from a hemlock, they slept in snow caves: a balm of good company to me. They made the state of Montana into a place that was not only cold, true, hard, and beautiful, but damn near humanly habitable. The young woman, now dead, was not herself a scientist but she was one of them in all other senses. She came from a town up on the High Line.

I had worked with her too, and seen her enliven long afternoons that could otherwise be just a tedious and not very lucrative form of self-demeanment. She was one of those rowdy, robust people—robust in good times, just as robust when she was angry or miserable—who are especially hard to imagine dead. She was a rascal of wit. She could be hilariously crude. We all knew her by her last name, because her first seemed too ladylike and demure. After the phone call to Helena, it took me a long time to make the mental adjustment of tenses: She had been a rascal of wit.

The memorial service was scheduled for such-and-such day, in that town up on the High Line.

We drove up together on winter roads, myself and two of the Helena friends, a husband-and-wife pair of plant ecologists. Others had gone ahead. Places available for sleeping, spare rooms and floors; make contact by phone; meet at the church. We met at the church and sat lumpish while a local pastor discoursed with transcendent irrelevance about what we could hardly recognize as her life and death. It wasn't his fault, he didn't know her. There was a reception with the family, followed by a post-wake on our own at a local bar, a fervent gathering of young survivors determined not only to cling to her memory but to cling to each other more appreciatively now that such a persuasive warning knell of mortality had been rung, and then sometime after dark as the wind came up and the temperature dropped away as though nothing was under it and a new storm raked in across those wheatlands, the three of us started driving back south. It had been my first trip to the High Line.

Aside from the note in the door, this is the part I remember most clearly. The car's defroster wasn't working. I had about four inches of open windshield. It was a little Honda that responded to wind like a shuttlecock, and on slick pavement the rear end flapped like the tail of a trout. We seemed to be rolling down a long dark tube coated inside with ice, jarred back and forth by the crosswinds, nothing else visible except the short tongue of road ahead and the streaming snow and the trucks blasting by too close in the other lane. How ironic, I thought, if we die on the highway while returning from a funeral. I hunched over the wheel, squinting out through that gap of windshield, until certain muscles in my right shoulder and neck shortened themselves into a knot. The two plant ecologists kept me awake with talk. One of them, from the back seat, worked at the knot in my neck. We talked about friendship and the message of death as we all three felt we had heard it, which was to cherish the living, while you have them. Seize, hold, appreciate. Pure friendship, uncomplicated by romance or blood, is one of the most nurturing human relationships and one of the most easily taken for granted. This was our consensus, spoken and unspoken.

These two plant ecologists had been my dear friends for a few years, but we were never closer than during that drive. Well after midnight, we reached their house in Helena. I slept on sofa cushions. In the morning they got me to a doctor for the paralytic clench in my neck. That was almost ten years ago and I've hardly seen them since.

The fault is mine, or the fault is nobody's. We got older and busier and trails diverged. They began raising children. I traveled to Helena less and less. Mortgages, serious jobs, deadlines; and the age of sleeping on sofa cushions seemed to have passed. I moved, they moved, opening more geographical distance. Montana is a big place and the roads are often bad. These facts offered in explanation sound even to me like excuses. The ashes of the young woman who slipped on the ice have long since been sprinkled onto a mountain top or into a river, I'm not sure which. Nothing to be done now either for her or about her. The two plant ecologists I still cherish, in intention anyway, at a regrettable distance, as I do a small handful of other precious friends, who seem to have disappeared from my life by wind erosion or melting.

3

Leontiev's Axiom

The ice mass of a mountain glacier flows down its valley in much the same complicated pattern as a river flowing in its bed. Obviously the glacier is much slower. Glacial ice may move at rates between six inches and six feet per day; river water may move a distance in that range every second. Like the water of a river, though, the ice of any particular glacier does not all flow at the same rate. There are eddies and tongues and slack zones, currents and swells, differential vectors of mix and surge. The details of the flow pattern depend on particularities to each given case: depth of the ice, slope, contour of the bed, temperature. But some generalizations can be made. Like a river, a glacier will tend to register faster flow rates at the surface than at depths, faster flows at midchannel than along the edges, and faster flows down toward the middle reaches than up near the source. One formula the scientists use to describe the relations between flow rate and those other factors is:

$$u = k_1 \sin^3 a\ h^4 + k_2 \sin^2 a\ h^2.$$

Everyone stay calm. This formula is not Leontiev's Axiom, and so we aren't going to bother deciphering it.

Turbulent flow is what makes a glacier unfathomable, in the sense of *fathoming* that connotes more than taking an ice-core measurement of depth. Turbulent flow is also what distinguishes a river from, say, a lake. When a river itself freezes, the complexities of turbulent flow interact with the peculiar physics of ice formation to produce a whole rat's nest of intriguing and sometimes inconvenient surprises. Because of turbulence, the water of a river cools down toward the freezing point uniformly, not in stratified layers as in a lake. Eventually the entire mass of flowing water drops below 32 degrees F. Small disks of ice, called frazil ice, then appear. Again because of turbulence, this frazil ice doesn't all float on the surface (despite being lighter than water) but mixes throughout the river's depth. Frazil ice has a tendency to adhesion, so some of it sticks to riverbed rocks. Some of it gloms onto bridge pilings and culverts, growing thick as a soft cold fur. Some of it aggregates with other frazil ice, forming large dollops of drifting slush. Meanwhile huge slabs of harder sheet ice, formed along the banks and broken free as the river changed level, may also be floating downstream. The slabs of sheet ice and the dollops of frazil ice go together like bricks and mortar. Stacking up at a channel constriction, they can lock themselves into an ice bridge.

Generally, when such an ice bridge forms, the river will have room to flow underneath. If the river is very shallow and the slabs of sheet ice are large, possibly not. Short of total blockage, the flow of the river will be slowed somewhat where it must pass through that narrowed gap; if it slows to less than a certain critical value, more ice will collect along the front face of the bridge and the ice cover will expand upstream. The relevant formula here is:

$$v_c = \left(1 - h/H\right) \sqrt{2g\left(p - p_i/p\right) h,}$$

where V_c is the critical flow rate and h is the ice thickness and everything else represents something too. But this also is not Leontiev's Axiom, and so we can ignore it, praise God.

The Madison River where it runs north through Montana happens to be very shallow. Upstream from (that is, south of) the lake that sits five miles north of Ennis, it is a magnificent stretch of habitat for stoneflies and caddisflies and trout and blue heron and fox and eagles and, half the year anyway, fishermen. The water is warmed at its geothermal source in Yellowstone Park, cooled again by its Montana tributaries like West Fork, rich in nutrients and oxygen, clear, lambent, unspoiled. Thanks to these graces, it is probably much too famous for its own good, and here I am making it a little more famous still. Upstream from the highway bridge at Ennis, where it can be conveniently floated by fishermen in rafts and guided Mackenzies, it gets an untoward amount of attention. This is where the notorious salmonfly hatch happens: boat traffic like the Henley Regatta, during that dizzy two weeks of June while the insects swarm and the fish gluttonize. This is the stretch of Madison for fishermen who crave trophies but not solitude. Downstream from the Ennis bridge it becomes a different sort of river. It becomes a different sort of place.

Downstream from the Ennis bridge, for that five-mile stretch to the lake, the Madison is a broken-up travesty of a river that offers mediocre fishing and clumsy floating and no trophy trout and not many salmonflies and I promise you fervently you wouldn't like it. This stretch is called "the channels." The river braids out into a maze of elbows and sloughs and streams separated by hundreds of small and large islands, some covered only with grass and willow, some shaded with buckling old-growth cottonwoods, some holding thickets of water birch and woods rose and raspberry scarcely tramped through by a single fisherman in the course of a summer. The deer love these islands and, in May, so do the nesting geese. Mosquitoes are bad here. The walking is difficult and there are bleached cottonwood deadfalls waiting to tear your waders. At the end of a long day's float, headwinds and choppy waves will come up on the lake just as you try to row your boat across to the ramp. Take my word, you'd hate the whole experience. Don't bother. Give it a miss. I adore that five miles of river more than any piece of landscape in the state of Montana.

Surrounding the braidwork of channels is a zone of bottomland roughly two miles wide, a great flat swath of sub-irrigated meadow only barely above the river's springtime high-water level. This low meadow area is an unusual sort of no-man's-land that performs a miraculous service: protecting the immediate riparian vicinity of the channels from the otherwise-inevitable arrival of ranch houses, summer homes, resort lodges, motels, all-weather roads, development, spoliation, and all other manner of venal doom. Tantalizing and vulnerable as it may appear on a July afternoon, the channels meadowland is an ideal place to raise bluegrass and Herefords and sandhill cranes but, for reasons we'll come to, is not really good for much else.

By late December the out-of-state fishermen are long gone, the duck hunters more recently, and during a good serious stretch of weather the dark river begins to flow gray and woolly with frazil ice. If the big slabs of sheet ice are moving too, a person can stand on the Ennis highway bridge and hear the two kinds of ice rubbing, hissing, whispering to each other as though in conspiracy toward mischief, or maybe revenge. (Through the three winters I lived in Ennis myself, I stood on that bridge often, gawking and listening. There aren't too many other forms of legal amusement in a Montana town of a thousand souls during the short days and long weeks of midwinter.) By this time the lake, five miles downstream, will have already frozen over. Then the river water cools still farther, the frazil thickens, the slabs bump and tumble into those narrow channels, until somewhere, at a point of constriction down near the lake, mortar meets brick and you begin to get:

$$v_c = \left(1 - h/H\right) \sqrt{2g\left(p - p_i/p\right)h}.$$

Soon the river is choked with its own ice. All the channels are nearly or totally blocked. But water is still arriving from upstream, and it has to go somewhere. So it flows out across the bottomland. It pours out over its banks and, moving quickly, faster than a man can walk, it covers a large part of that meadow area with water. Almost as quickly, the standing floodwater becomes ice.

If you have been stubborn or foolish enough to build your house out on that flat, on a pretty spot at the edge of the river, you now have three feet of well-deserved ice in your living room. "Get back away from me," is what the river has told you. "Show some goddamn respect." There are memories of this sort of ice-against-man encounter. It hasn't happened often, that a person should come along so mule-minded as to insist on flouting the reality of the ice, but often enough for a few vivid exempla. Back in 1863, for instance, a settler named Andrew Odell, who had built his cabin out on the channel meadows, woke up one night in December to find river water already lapping onto his bed. He grabbed his blanket and fled, knee deep, toward higher ground on the far side of a spring creek that runs parallel to the channels a half mile east. That spring creek is now called Odell Creek, and it marks a rough eastern boundary of the zone that gets buried in ice. Nowadays you don't see any cabins or barns in the flat between Odell Creek and the river.

Folks in Ennis call this salubrious event the Gorge. The Gorge doesn't occur every year, and it isn't uniform or predictable when it does. Two or three winters may go by without serious weather, without a Gorge, without that frozen flood laid down upon thousands of acres, and then there will come a record year. A rancher named Ralph Paugh remembers one particular Gorge, because it back-flooded all the way up across Odell to fill his barn with a two-foot depth of ice. This was on Christmas Day, 1983. "It come about four o'clock," he recalls. "Never had got to the barn before." His barn has sat on that rise since 1905. He has some snapshots from the 1983 episode, showing vistas and mounds of whiteness. "That pile there, see, we piled that up with the dozer when we cleaned it out." Ralph also remembers talk about the Gorge in 1907, the year he was born; that one took out the old highway bridge, so for the rest of the winter schoolchildren and mailmen and whoever else had urgent reason for crossing the river did so on a trail of planks laid across ice. The present bridge is a new one, the lake north of Ennis is also a relatively recent contrivance (put there for hydroelectric generation about when Ralph Paugh was a baby), but the Gorge of the Madison channels is natural and immemorial.

I used to lace up my Sorels and walk on it. Cold sunny afternoons of January or February, bare willows, bare cottonwoods, exquisite solitude, fox tracks in an inch of fresh snow, and down through three feet of ice below my steps and the fox tracks were spectacular bits of Montana that other folk, outlanders, coveted only in summer.

Mostly I wandered these places alone. Then one year a certain biologist of my recent acquaintance came down for a visit in Ennis. I think this was in late April. I know that the river had gorged that year and that the ice was now melting away from the bottomland, leaving behind its moraine of fertile silt. The channels themselves, by now, were open and running clear. The first geese had arrived. This biologist and I spent that day in the water, walking downriver through the channels. We didn't fish. We didn't collect aquatic insects or study the nesting of *Branta canadensis*. The trees hadn't yet come into leaf and it was no day for a picnic. We just walked in the water, stumbling over boulders, bruising our feet, getting wet over the tops of our waders. We saw the Madison channels, fresh from cold storage, before anyone else that year. We covered only about three river miles in the course of the afternoon, but that was enough to exhaust us, and then we stumbled out across the muddy fields and walked home on the road. How extraordinary, I thought, to come across a biologist who would share my own demented appreciation for such an arduous, stupid, soggy trek. So I married her.

The channels of the Madison River are a synecdoche. They are the part that resonates so as to express the significance of the whole. To understand how I mean that, it might help to know Leontiev's Axiom. Konstantin Leontiev was a cranky Russian thinker from the last century. He trained as a physician, worked as a diplomat in the Balkans, wrote

novels and essays that aren't read much today, and at the end of his life
flirted with becoming a monk. By most of the standards you and I likely
share, he was an unsavory character. But even a distempered and retro-
grade Czarist of monastic leanings is right about something once in a
while.

Leontiev wrote: "To stop Russia from rotting, one would have to put it
under ice."

In my mind, in my dreams, that great flat sheet of Madison River
whiteness spreads out upon the whole state of Montana. I believe, with
Leontiev, in salvation by ice.

4

Sources

The biologist whose husband I am sometimes says to me: "All right, so
where do we go when Montana's been ruined? Alaska? Norway?
Where?" This is a dark joke between us. She grew up in Montana, loves
the place the way some women might love an incorrigibly self-destructive
man, with pain and fear and pity, and she has no desire to go anywhere
else. I grew up in Ohio, discovered home in Montana only fifteen years
ago, and I feel the same. But still we play at the dark joke. "Not Norway," I say, "and you know why." We're each half Norwegian and
we've actually eaten lutefisk. "How about Antarctica," I say. "Antarctica should be okay for a while yet."

On the desk before me now is a pair of books about Antarctica. Also
here are a book on the Arctic, another book titled *The World of Ice,* a
book of excerpts from Leontiev, a master's thesis on the subject of goose
reproduction and water levels in the Madison channels, an extract from
an unpublished fifty-year-old manuscript on the history of Ennis, Montana, a cassette tape of a conversation with Ralph Paugh, and a fistful of
photocopies of technical and not-so-technical articles. One of the less
technical articles is titled "Ice on the World," from a recent issue of

National Geographic. In this article is a full-page photograph of strawberry plants covered with a thick layer of ice.

These strawberry plants grew in central Florida. They were sprayed
with water, says the caption, because sub-freezing temperatures had
been forecast. The growers knew that a layer of ice, giving insulation,
even giving up some heat as the water froze, would save them.

In the foreground is one large strawberry. The photocopy shows it
dark gray, but in my memory it's a death-defying red.

2 QUESTS

RIVER HISTORY

Gretel Ehrlich

It's morning in the Absaroka Mountains. The word *absaroka* means "raven" in the Crow language, though I've seen no ravens in three days. Last night I slept with my head butted against an Engelmann spruce and on waking the limbs looked like hundreds of arms swinging in a circle. The trunk is bigger than an elephant's leg, bigger than my torso. I stick my nose against the bark. Tiny opals of sap stick to my cheeks and the bark breaks up, textured: red and gray, coarse and smooth, wet and flaked.

A tree is an aerial garden, a botanical migration from the sea, from those earliest plants, the seaweeds; it is a purchase on crumbled rock, on ground. The human, standing, is only a different upsweep and articulation of cells. How treelike we are, how human the tree.

But I've come here to seek out the source of a river and as we make the daylong ascent from a verdant valley, I think about walking and wilderness. We use the word "wilderness," but perhaps we mean wildness. Isn't that why I've come here? In wilderness, I seek the wildness in myself—and in so doing, come on the wildness everywhere around me because, after all, being part of nature, I'm cut from the same cloth.

Following the coastline of a lake, I watch how wind picks up water in dark blasts and drops it again. Ducks glide in Vs away from me, out onto the fractured, darkening mirror. I stop. A hatch of mayflies powders the air and the archaic, straight-winged dragonflies hang, blunt-nosed, above me. A friend talks about aquatic bugs: water beetles, spinners, assassin bugs, and one that hatches, mates, and dies in a total lifespan of two hours. At the end of the meadow the lake drains into a fast-moving creek. I quicken my pace and trudge upward. Walking is also an ambulation of mind. The human armour of bones rattle, fat rolls, and inside this durable, fleshy prison of mine, I make a beeline toward otherness, lightness, or, maybe like a moth, toward flame.

Somewhere along the trail I laugh out loud. How shell-like the body seems suddenly—not fleshy at all, but inhuman and hard. And farther up, I step out of my body though I'm still held fast by something, but what? I don't know.

How foolish the preparations for wilderness trips seem now. We pour over our maps, chart our expeditions. We "gear up" at trailheads with pitons and crampons, horsepacks and backpacks, fly rods and cameras, forgetting the meaning of simply going, of lifting thought-covers, of disburdenment. I look up from these thoughts. A blue heron rises from a gravel bar and glides behind a gray screen of dead trees, appears in an opening where an avalanche downed pines, and lands again on water.

I stop to eat lunch. Ralph Waldo Emerson wrote, "The Gautama said that the first men ate the earth and found it sweet." I eat baloney and cheese and think about eating the earth. It's another way of framing our wonder in which the width of the mouth stands for the generous palate of consciousness. I cleanse my palate with miner's lettuce and streamwater and try to imagine what kinds of sweetness the earth provides: the taste of glacial flour, or the mineral taste of basalt, the fresh and foul bouquets of rivers, the dessicated, stinging flavor of a snowstorm—like eating red ants, my friend says.

As I begin to walk again it occurs to me that this notion of "eating the earth" is not about gluttony, hedonism, or sin, but, rather, unconditional love. Everywhere I look I see the possibility of love. To find wildness, I must first offer myself up, accept all that comes before me: a bullfrog breathing hard on a rock; moose tracks under elk scats; a cloud that looks like a clothespin; a seep of water from a high cirque, black on brown rock, draining down from the brain of the world.

At treeline, birdsong stops. I'm lifted into another movement of music, one with no particular notes, only windsounds becoming watersounds, becoming windsounds. Above, a cornice crowns a ridge and melts into a teal and turquoise lake, like a bladder, leaking its wine.

On top of Marston Pass I'm in a ruck of steep valleys and gray, treeless peaks. The alpine carpet, studded with red paintbrush and alpine buttercups, gives way to rock. Now all the way across a vertiginous valley, I see where water oozes from moss and mud, how, at its source, it quickly becomes something else.

Emerson also said: "Every natural fact is an emanation, and that from which it emanates is an emanation also, and from every emanation is a new emanation." The ooooze, the source of a great river, is now a white chute tumbling over soft folds of conglomerate rock. Wind tears at it, throwing sheets of water to another part of the mountainside; soft earth gives way under my feet, clouds spill upward and spit rain. Isn't everything redolent with loss, with momentary radiance, a coming to different ground? Stone basins catch the waterfall, spill it again, like thoughts strung together, laddered down.

I see where meltwater is split by a rock—half going west to the Pacific, the other going east to the Atlantic, for this is the Continental Divide. Down the other side the air I gulp feels softer. Ice spans and tunnels the creek, then, when night comes but before the full moon, falling stars have the same look as that white chute of water, falling against the rock of night.

To rise above treeline is to go above thought and after, the descent back into birdsong, bog orchids, willows, and firs is to sink into the pre-literate parts of ourselves. It is to forget discontent, undisciplined needs. Here the world is only space, raw loneliness, green valleys hung vertically. Losing myself to it—if I can—I do not fall . . . or, if I do, I'm only another cataract of water.

Wildness has no conditions, no sure routes, no peaks or goals, no source that is not instantly becoming something more than itself, then letting go of that, always becoming. It cannot be stripped to its complexity by cat scan or telescope. Rather, it is a many-pointed truth, almost a bluntness, a sudden essence like the wild strawberries strung along the ground on scarlet runners under my feet. Wildness is source and fruition at once, as if every river circled round, the mouth eating the tail—and the tail, the source.

Now I am camped among trees again. Four yearling moose, their chestnut coats shiny from a summer's diet of willow shoots, tramp past my bedroll and drink from a spring that issues sulphurous water. The ooze, the white chute, the narrow stream—now almost a river—joins this small spring and slows into skinny oxbows and deep pools before breaking again on rock, a stepladder of sequined riffles.

To trace the history of a river, or a raindrop, as John Muir would have done, is also to trace the history of the soul, the history of the mind descending and arising in the body. In both, we constantly seek and stumble on divinity, which, like the cornice feeding the lake and the spring becoming a waterfall, feeds, spills, falls, and feeds itself over and over again.

THE GATEKEEPERS

Beth Ferris

It was early morning and the light around the pass looked solid enough to hold a falling body. Something startled the goats, perhaps a bear or a lion. One by one, they launched themselves off the cliff and hung suspended for a long moment above a thousand feet of dense, blue space. They might have been white birds in the circle of my binoculars, buoyed up by the momentum of their leap. As they caught themselves on a narrow ledge, they ran the rockface in a line, white bodies shimmering like a mirage. The way they moved was something to believe in; falling was not a concept they knew or feared. We put down our binoculars, and began our long climb.

I braced myself against a rock while Ursula hoisted my pack—sixty pounds of camera gear and a summer's worth of food—onto my back. I did her the same favor. Our packs felt like straightjackets; the final click of the waist belt locked us in. Ursula wobbled a step or two, then found balance; her calves swelled every stride. I'd hired Ursula, a young zoology student, to help me make a film about mountain goats on Gunsight Pass, in Glacier Park. We were glad to be moving. For two weeks, we'd camped in a boggy alpine meadow waiting for the avalanche that blocked the Gunsight trail to melt out. Just the day before, a Park Ranger told us

BETH FERRIS

to postpone our climb until the trail crew dynamited a route through the snowslide. Every night dampness seeped up through the tent floor. The blackflies and mosquitos were so thick we couldn't pick them out of our rice with a fork. Besides, I was too obsessed to wait longer. It was already late June, and I needed footage of young goats, still spark-eyed with insolence.

The Gunsight trail slashed back and forth across a vertical cliff, slippery with meltwater and ice. This presented particular danger to the one carrying the tripod—an ungainly, cranky piece of equipment—lashed on top of her pack. The tripod's sharp little feet stuck out a foot and a half, snagging at the rock where the trail narrowed. We traded off frequently, and tottered up the trail like women on bound feet.

Toward noon, a wall of blue ice stared us in the face. An avalanche that lasts into summer is a treacherous affair. Meltwater rivers eat out caverns under the surface, hidden by a thin bridge of snow. Huge crevices, dark with dirt and debris, gape open where the snowslide's weight has shifted. At any moment, the ice can break along these faultlines; with a crack like sonic boom, huge slabs of snow hurtle into emptiness. As one crosses such an avalanche, the familiar vertigo of daily life is compressed into small moments, exquisite with terror.

We hacked footholds in the granular surface with bright orange ice axes; ice particles flew up and glittered. One foot, then another inched onto the hand-carved ledge. I dug my fingers into the harsh snow, and hewed another set of steps. The avalanche was not far across, perhaps a hundred yards. But it already seemed too late to turn around. It was our fate to walk a glass roof, tilting gradually toward us at an ever-steeper angle. We were hypnotized, I think, because I didn't feel my bloody fingers until afterward. The snowslide fell away so absolutely that there was nothing at all below us. The earth had vanished; all I saw was snow and blue sky. Dizzy with the sensation that sky lay both above and beneath me, I fought the urge to drop everything and run blind. I knew how fear always made me hurry as though the future could leave me behind. I forced myself to slow down.

74

By the time we crawled the last switchback, the pass lay in the heavy shadow of mountains rising on either side. A large male goat appeared above us on a shockingly red boulder, a spear of light catching his fur. I knew it was a little far-fetched to imagine him the gatekeeper, but the way he eyed us as we threw off our packs was unsettling. He slowly absorbed our presence, and the odd things we had brought into the blackness of his eyes. Close up, he had the bearded, cryptic face of a Chinese Patriarch. It seemed the whole world could fall into those eyes and he would not be shaken. Nietzsche said that if you stare into the abyss, it stares back at you. This is rather like a goat's gaze: no coldness there, but a certain impartiality. The eyes were unreadable, so we saw ourselves in them.

The other goats were gone, but their pungent, musky smell rose from the rocks. They had pawed deep beds in loose dirt under Krummholz groves, and scratched their backs on the dwarfed and twisted branches—strung now with their hair like oddly decorated Christmas trees. Over the years, their feet had woven a network of tiny trails through meadows and across rockslides, worn even into rock itself, the whole pass carved into an artifact of their civilization. Another intelligence was at work here; we were strangers from a distant culture. It was like coming across the stone men Inuits build to interrupt the vacant tundra; we would never understand the world behind these symbols. But we might look through them and guess at their meaning, wondering at the relation to ourselves.

Dark brought a sudden chill, as if cold were the nature of the pass, masked all day by the sun's warmth. We shivered in our sweaty shirts, greedily combing goat hair from the branches for a weaving Ursula was making. The Kwakiutl and Tlingit, Northwest Coast Indians, used to weave goat fur with a weft of cedar strips into dense, watertight capes and blankets. I jammed some hair in my pocket, like a talisman. When I was five or six, I had a passion for arrowheads washed ashore at our lake place. I kept my pockets full of quartz and agates, and when I ran out of arrowhead luck, threw one of these stones into the lake and made a deal: give me an arrowhead and I'll give you the prettiest stone I have. I was on the verge of making a similar deal with the shadowy emptiness around the pass.

In a smooth, courtly leap, our goat abandoned us, slipped away across a rockslide. Loneliness that comes with day's end in the high mountains fell. In the blueness, waves of mountains glowed with a momentary, incandescent flush. The light lingering in the valley seemed irretrievable, and a familiar loss, cold and frightening, yawned open. All day, I'd foolishly thought my fears would evaporate once we reached the pass; knowing constant motion keeps fear at bay. But now I was too exhausted to move. Match after match flared from my numb hands while deepening cold nudged under my shirt. The clarity of failure flashed with each burst of light. I was twenty-four, my marriage falling apart; had never finished college; had no idea what to do with the life stretching ahead like a minefield. After three years following my husband around the Montana wilderness studying mountain goats, this film of my own was a desperate act of self retrieval.

A tentative flame wavered in the gas ring of the primus stove. All I needed was a good meal and confidence would fill me like hot soup. Once the light flared, though, everything outside its circle grew darker and farther away. Ursula emerged from the shadows as I dumped pellets of freeze-dried food into steaming water. Leaning over to pull a sierra cup from my pack, my leg hit the stove, knocking it sideways. Our dinner steamed out into the rocks and dirt.

Quickly, I scooped up congealed fragments of potatoes and gravy and held the cup out for Ursula to see. She picked out a stone with her spoon; we laughed a little.

Wandering out into the dark to refill the pot with water cascading down a cliff, I wondered if clumsiness and confusion could be permanent—a chronic illness. Mustering all my concentration, I avoided falling on the wet rocks, and my slippery mind settled on the solid and practical: getting the water back to the stove. The goats survived in this wind-carved zone of thumbnail plants—the only large mammals to winter on these mountaintops, pawing for food in thigh-deep snow. All inessentials

scoured away, they lived at the extreme edge of possibility. No wonder
the ice-clear vision in their eyes—perhaps some of it would rub off.

By midsummer we adopted the habit of bedding with the goats after
they finished feeding, and we had run through a couple hundred feet of
film. At Gunsight, the goats let us within ten or fifteen feet; over the
years they'd developed a craving for salts in human urine. It's disturbing
at first to have a goat eye you greedily every time you drop your pants.
But despite the beggarliness, the goats maintained an elegant solitude, a
self-contained privacy like a shell. A forefoot flung over the chasm below, they spent hours every day staring into the spaces between mountains. Their dark eyes never hesitated, never released their pure,
resolute stare.

One morning, a curious and insecure yearling—she had been cast out
by the new kid in the family—got up from her bed and walked toward
us. Settling her delicate hooves on the watermarked rock, she stared with
eyes both hard as obsidian and yielding as water. I couldn't say what
drew her closer; perhaps a hazy recognition struck her suddenly, perhaps
it was simply curiosity. I shut my eyes, listening to the scratch of her
hoof pads on limestone. Her soft, damp nose brushed my face, my eyelids, and her rapid breathing lifted the hair on my forehead. When I
opened my eyes, she was gone.

She flopped down beside her mother, and looked back across an invisible barrier. A chasm had re-opened between us. I looked to Ursula for
reassurance. But Ursula, grown careless as a goat, leaned far over the
cliff edge, her eyes holding the mountains and valleys with a delicacy
and abstraction I could not follow.

There always was a secretiveness to the goats. Often they left the
pass and didn't come back for days. Ursula and I made our beds on a
narrow ledge under a steep cliff, comforted by our own artifacts: a burnt
pot, a cup, a notebook, jackets draped over rocks. In contrast to
the goats' whimsical departures, we were hidebound, strapped to the

materials of survival. Sometimes I insisted we drag our camera gear up a trail-less mountain to see where they had gone. But this was futile. We were far too burdened ever to catch up; once moving, the goats kept moving.

We were left with nothing to do but wait for their return. My eyes slid constantly over the landscape, hoping to be snagged by motion. One day, focused on a fly buzzing in a yellow-dot saxifrage at my feet, its face loomed larger and larger and everything else dropped out of sight. My normal sense of time, grazed off in minutes, went out the back door like a fast-talking salesman. Time and silence give sight fluency. Days or hours passed in a half-focused drowse, not really watching anything at all, but the light that hung around the land. My vision caught anything that moved at the periphery of its curve; a red-tail hawk before it slammed out of the sky on a hapless ground squirrel, an eagle's wing-shadow floating over the meadow. Eyes loose and unjointed, free in their sockets; the land shivered with expectancy—anything could move or happen at any time. More than once, a snowpatch turned out to be a goat that got up and walked away.

Our eyes were alert as a predator's, but anxious as prey. Looking all day for invisible goats, dark rocks that might be grizzly bears shifted in an eye's blink. Grizzlies lived in a place of fear tucked not far under the surface. We performed our little rituals: burning every can to kill the odor, hoisting food and garbage high in a tree far from camp. We knew we couldn't kill our female scent. At night on our stony ledge, we jumped every time a rock clattered or wind scraped the branches of a tree. To calm ourselves, we passed a flask of rum between us and talked about men.

One night, I finally fell into a restless sleep. In my dream, I was chasing the goats again, up a mountain in light so heavy my body seemed weighted with stones. A veil fell over my eyes, I couldn't open my eyelids wide enough to see clearly. The goats were suddenly in front of me, disturbingly unafraid. I knew instantly they were not goats at all. But what were they? I sensed obsession; one of my heart's

PHOTOGRAPHS

IN THE LANDSCAPE

John Smart

Landscapes

I began to photograph Montana about fifteen years ago. As a visitor, I was drawn to the unusually austere and bittersweet beauty of the open land. The vast exterior of the high plains and mountains had a poetic quality that was brutally honest yet intimate. As a resident, I continued to travel through a variety of landforms that were expansive, rolling, rising, and descending. The sky was animated and the wind rarely stopped. The landscape was creating an internal dialogue that needed to be worked out visually.

The first photographs I attempted were little more than topographic notations. Intuitively, I knew it would be difficult to define the images that seemed to be possible. My perceptions of the landscape were changing like vague wind clouds. I wasn't ready, but kept looking and taking in sensations of space and distance, while reading the contours of the land, patterns of light, and movements of the sky. It was important to improvise and learn to be graceful with the fairly rough elements at hand. I also needed to understand more about the ordinary as well as extraordinary places. Every so often, I would make a good picture and scream into the wind.

Elusive relationships eventually began to fall into place. Dynamics between the land and sky appeared in bold and subtle ways. Places that had seemed empty began to offer new images. Composition became a matter of responding to patterns of energy that could be arranged within a limited photographic frame. I accepted that the land was not an object to be possessed or controlled with the camera. I stepped aside and allowed the landscape to speak for itself. Insights and impressions that had been gathering for years were becoming integrated. The photographs were beginning to belong to the landscape.

Rangeland near Wolf Creek   1987

Near Ashland after a spring rain   1977

Looking south by Ingomar   1987

Cattle and the Crazy Mountains, north of Big Timber   1987

The Cayuse Livestock Company by the Crazy Mountains   1987

Sheep on the Cooney Ranch, south of Harlowton   *1987*

Windclouds near Porcupine Butte, Melville   1987

Dry creekbed and ranch north of Grassrange   1987

Sage and pine near Jackson, The Big Hole   1982

Looking northeast near Grassrange   1987

Dryland wheatfield north of Three Forks   1987

The Big Belt Mountains from the Helena Valley 1983

Road through Sweetgrass County   1987

Along the Rocky Mountain front, west of Augusta   1988

The Garden Wall, Glacier National Park   1987

Looking south near Springdale towards the Absaroka Range   1988

Madison River valley and the Madison Range by Ennis   1988

The Scratchgravel Hills by Silver City   1988

Looking west to the Continental Divide, near Canyon Creek   1988

Rivers

While working or travelling in different regions of Montana, I occasionally took the time to go fishing. Actually, the fish were only an excuse for being by a river. The rivers seemed to belong to the sky as they flowed directly from mountains. I would roll up my pants and step into the current, wondering how long it would take the water to reach the Mississippi Delta. My gym shoes sloshed with cold water as my legs became heavy and slightly numb. Standing still and gazing at the continuous motion of the river surface, I was very detached. The fishing was fantastic.

The Bitterroot River between Hamilton and Darby   1987

The Madison River near Quake Lake   1987

The Madison River near Cameron   1987

The Yellowstone River in the Paradise Valley near Emigrant   1987

The Missouri breaks and Missouri River, C.M. Russell Wildlife Refuge   1987

Bars

I took an interest in historic bars while photographing the Montana landscape. I was initially attracted to an atmosphere of authenticity that the vintage bars still retained. But as I came to know these places better, I discovered a unique social landscape. Each bar was a world of its own, with a distinct sense of community and an identity that appeared to be a combination of truth and myth. As the photographs progressed, I realized there was a connection between the landscape and the tradition of bars in the West. The man-made interior was a refuge from the immense and demanding exterior world.

The Montana Bar, Miles City   1977

Entering the New Atlas Bar, Columbus   1979

The New Atlas Bar, Columbus   1979

The Jersey Lilly Bar and Cafe, Ingomar   1981

own knots lay close at hand. A large male goat arched his back and stared at me, eyes swimming with strange light. Bewitched, I stepped closer, reached for him. But the goat already showed my darkest nature. The skin peeled away gradually from his face, and out came the long, pointed snout of a white bear. The bear's body shuddered and burst free of the goat, towering, monstrous above me. I was now the hunted one, though it took a second too long to figure this out. The bear understood torturous anticipation; he licked his paws slowly and let me run. My legs churned down the mountain, but all the while I stayed in one place. The light grew even dimmer, flickering like a candle. He caught me, wedged under a rock, and dragged me out with paws smelling faintly of musk.

I hated dreams that left me sweating with fear, and worse, mulling how quickly innocence could change to threat. I dimly understood the relationship between terror and seduction—the seductiveness of danger.

One morning we packed our gear and headed out for the glacier on the far side of the mountain.

We followed a shallow path in fist-size scree, steadying ourselves with ice axes as shards of pink-and-turquoise shale slipped into space.

We rarely talked while hiking; the wind filled my head with a crazy, wordless language. The glacier had ground the mountain down to a moonscape where nothing grew. An acid-blue lake shook and wavered in the light, but the land was starved as a desert. Blinded by the stony brightness, near-deaf from constant wind, my legs began to rise and fall without my participation. I flashed in and out of blackness, as though falling asleep or going under an anaesthetic. It was time to get out of the sun and eat something. We squeezed into a sheltered niche, on a cliff above a snowfield, and listened to the wind. It might have been the exertion of the climb, the altitude, or my thick fear departing, but as I sat against the warm rock my body seemed to shear off and drop away. Time slowed to underwater speed. Laboriously, I opened and closed my hand, fascinated to find it attached to my arm. The scarred landscape below glittered with startling clarity. I must have slept.

Ursula shook me and pointed—a band of goats had rounded the cliff edge just below us. We knew from the nanny with half a horn they were the goats from the Pass. Ursula grabbed the tripod and I fumbled to attach it to the camera. One of the kids, a clownish twin, charged a yearling in mock battle. Yearlings have little patience, particularly with young goats; he whirled and butted the kid off the cliff. The kid fell through the air, a startled expression in his black marble eyes, and jarred against the snowfield twenty feet below. He was stunned only for a second, then a joyful fury took over. He leapt up and down three times, stiff-legged, standing in one place, and threw himself down the glacier, bucking, rearing, head-tossing. The other goats could not resist; it was startling to see them catch his glee. Even the old nanny with half a horn hurtled herself off the cliff, body twisted in a dancing arc before she landed. Slashing the snow with her good horn, she charged everyone in her path. Energy flashed through the herd; playfulness at the core of each body radiated from muscle to muscle. This was the essence of freedom. This was laughter.

The goats whirled on like Sufi dancers. At the bottom of the snowslide, the pulse subsided. They were different creatures now, led by the sedate old nanny across the cliff; they'd left their true story entwined in skid marks on the snow.

Fall arrived like a sadness one is never prepared for. The wind dropped. As daytime and evening temperatures leveled out, we entered a period of profound silence. No longer did we jump out of our sleeping bags as the hard-edged sun scraped through the mountains. Hauling out of the warmth of our beds was like breaking a thin layer of ice.

The sense of urgency had gone quietly and left a vacuum in its wake. Sometimes we followed the goats without cameras, just to see where they had gone; joking about the lightness of bodies that could blow off cliffs with no burden to weight them down.

One perfectly clear, still fall day, a day that stretched into an eternity of blue light, we hiked farther than we intended. The sun cast giant shadows beyond our bodies as we climbed back down the ridge toward camp.

We could not quite penetrate the hazy duskiness around us and, careless with hunger and fatigue, paid no attention to our surroundings. Crossing a field of horse-size boulders, something that wasn't wind chilled the back of my neck. A boulder shifted slightly. We slid to a stop—two hundred yards away, a sow grizzly and her yearling twins materialized. They fed on lomatium and avalanche lily roots, slowly stripping the earth from a rocky ledge as though separating flesh from bone. The landscape slid out of whack: the grizzly loomed monstrous, close, then far away again, swaying back and forth on monumental thighs.

Crinkling her small eyes in our direction, combing the air with her paws, she scratched her nose, a nose sensitive to any molecule of carrion. A clear image of our half-eaten can of sardines, wrapped up in my pack, appeared. I could hear my heart, and thought I heard Ursula's thud against her chest.

I put my hand on her arm. We began to crawl slowly backward. There were only more boulders behind us, no escape, no trees, yet—and this surprised me—I knew that it would be all right. Maybe I sensed the bear's half-hearted interest in us. But I think I passed through a barrier just then—the way one accepts one's self, the end of summer, or a death.

The sow dropped to her forepaws; abruptly as if insulted, she whirled and sloped away, the cubs bumbling behind. Ursula and I looked at one another with wordless joy. In a moment of grace, the place I had lived all summer had come to live in me.

We ran down through the shadowy boulders, panting like children playing a last game of tag before dark. We hit the scree slope, glissading effortlessly in ankle-deep stones. Then the bones in my legs gave up all effort of holding me together. My joints loosened, my knees buckled and gave way, and I lurched forward, clutching air. Struggling for control, I fell over a small stone, flipped backward, and lay flailing my arms like a beetle. I heard Ursula laugh as she approached. Then I laughed. She gave me her hand and pulled me up. All the way down the mountain, our laughter was louder than the clatter of stones we sent scurrying away from our feet. There we were, skittering through dark, not falling, but stumbling and bouncing back upright like those round-bottomed dolls you can't push over.

THIRTY PRETTY GOOD YEARS

Charles F. Waterman

This happened at Clyde Park, Montana, in the late fifties. It is not likely to happen today for times and attitudes have changed, even in Montana—but I can think of no other place it could have happened, even in the fifties or earlier.

We were new to Montana then, not new to mountain country but still aware of broad space, of wind-torn cumulus clouds and scattered mountain ranges seemingly carelessly spaced and not quite hidden behind horizons.

The Crazy Mountains don't exactly loom over Clyde Park, being miles away, but any visitor is likely to be conscious of them because they are set far apart from other ranges and they seem to shove abruptly upward from rolling hills. From Clyde Park you don't really notice the benches and foothills and you simply look at the peaks, which are a little forbidding. Writers often speak of "brooding mountains" and if mountains brood, the Crazies certainly do.

We stopped at a filling station in Clyde Park and the man in charge started the pump at thirty-some cents a gallon. I gawked at the Crazies.

"They tell me there are mountain goats over there," I said. "Is there any way we can see one?"

CHARLES F. WATERMAN

At the time I was pretty tied up in big-game hunting and I had never seen a mountain goat. The man on the gasoline pump said there were goats there all right but it was a little hard to get to them.

"You really need horses," he said. "You need to get about seven miles from the road and maybe climb some after that."

I tried to be clever. I said I didn't happen to have any horses with me. He smiled a little.

"Oh, I have horses," he said as the pump registered two dollars and something. "I'm not using them. Take mine."

"Well," I said (still being cute) "I'd have to get them to the end of the road and the back seat is already full."

"Oh, that's no problem," he said. "Take my stock truck. I'm not using it."

He nodded toward it, parked beside the station. It was shiny and looked new.

At three dollars and something the gas pump clicked off.

"What would that goat trip cost us?" I asked.

The station man looked a little hurt.

"Oh, it wouldn't cost you anything," he said. "I'm not using that stuff."

Remember that was in the fifties and it was the next year when we stopped at the Husky station in Bozeman. We were driving a new GMC Carryall we'd sacrificed for. It was full of camping gear because we were going both hunting and fishing. When the pump read a dollar and something the attendant, whom I'd never seen before, asked if we were going hunting and we said we were.

"Come and hunt with us," he said. "We've got a camp on Freezeout Mountain. We generally have some elk."

I asked if he did guiding himself. By then the pump read two-eighty.

"Oh, no," he said. "We don't do any guiding. We just have this big cabin and there's lots of room."

Now such things haven't happened in Montana lately and, of course, the out-of-stater is now recognized for what he is, carrying tourist dollars,

84

and of course there are Montanans who recognize him mainly for that, but there was that special attitude in those days. I am sure we would have been permanently attracted to Montana anyway, but we were awed by the friendliness—so disturbed by it in fact that we were occasionally struck dumb by it, unable to handle an offer of a pack train and stock truck for free on an acquaintance of less than three minutes. And now we are afraid nobody will believe those stories.

We weren't city folks ourselves, and although I had ridden freight trains through the West during the Great Depression we thought of Montana as a sort of hunting and fishing frontier. On our first trip from Florida we stopped in Denver, where we'd once lived, and bought some fishing gear for the Montana wilds, then discovered that even then some of the finest tackle shops were located on the scene. We arrived in Livingston and rented an upstairs apartment for $25 a month. The Yellowstone was muddy and we went to the Madison where we happened to strike a salmonfly hatch at just the right time and we caught bright brown trout and camped alone on a rocky flat. The trout were bigger than we'd ever expected and my wife Debie tied a big special fly that had more of everything than the standard salmonfly patterns.

We fished every day that summer and early fall and we were on the Madison when the antelope season opened, and late one evening with the sun gone behind the Gravellys a single big pronghorn buck, evidently moved by hunters from a better area, loped purposefully across our flat and disappeared in the distance with surprising speed. Next year, I said, we'd get big-game licenses. Then, in my first and only venture into graffiti, I chiseled my initial on a rock beside the Madison, feeling a little silly after I'd done it, and we went back to Florida, entrapped by the Montana country and destined to come back each year for more than thirty.

I hunted elk with a pistol, a dream I'd had for years, and when I'd finally scored that way we turned to mule deer and sought big bucks each season, often saving our tags until the last few days. It was the late fall that intrigued us most, the time when bucks gathered their harems, and we hunted from snowy ridges with binoculars and spotting scopes, studying the slopes and looking for the capital Y made by a doe's ears as she bedded in the sage—and once the capital Y was located we would see other deer there and hopefully a big buck in charge. We even met rutting bucks that shook their heads and raked saplings when they saw us— bucks that had learned no fear of man yet, even in 1960, but we listened to veteran hunters who had seen a day when a single deer track would lead a hunter on a lung-bursting chase.

We began our hunting at a time when the mule deer population was high and few native hunters walked far from their cars to collect venison. The whitetail population was low and it was hard to believe ancients who swore that there had been a time when the muleys were scarce and whitetails plentiful. And then by 1987 the whitetails had come back to the brushy bottoms and ranchers' yards and the warlike bucks were driving off the muleys.

"Those whitetails are more efficient," we said. "They run instead of bouncing and don't always look back at top of the ridge."

There were bonuses with deer hunting, the surprising appearance of a crumbling cabin in what had appeared to be a wilderness canyon, a long abandoned homestead with old dreams, joys, and disappointments, gradually being reclaimed by weeds and woods—and only after it was found would we notice the overgrown trail that led to it and had been followed by buckboards and creaking wagons. Nearly always there was the wonderment at how anyone had lived there in winter and the comment that it must have been a long way to town in those days. And as we went farther up the canyon where deer tracks seemed to funnel toward some mysterious objective we'd sometimes find still another cabin—or possibly the faint outline of one's foundation and the sparkle of some long-shattered bit of glass in the weeds. Long way to town.

And there was the time near Lima when the late fall snowstorm closed in and we grinningly went away and left a dozen big bucks with their several harems in a little canyon—no time to drag one out as the trails closed. And down on the border of the Madison Valley when I waited tensely for a really big buck to work his way up into the Madison Range, finally settling the crosshairs behind his shoulder, only to have him drop away from them, and I finally heard a shot from what seemed a distant ridge, after which my wife Debie walked down from there—a small red-shirted figure who had collected a number of big bucks. And all these years later I look up at four sets of mounted antlers and cannot remember which of us each set belongs to without looking at the little brass tags on the plaques.

There were fish and game problems then, as there are now. There was the constant demand for dams across Montana's trout streams and the heated meetings when developers and nature lovers argued the merits of lakes and free-flowing rivers with both sides sometimes screaming impudently.

There was the business of fish hatcheries and planted trout and when we first came to Montana it was easy to stand near the tracks of a hatchery truck and catch a foot-long rainbow on every cast of a dry fly. But the serious fishermen wanted wild fish and the advocates of "tourist fish" finally accepted the principles of stream management. So eventually, catch-and-release became the religion of serious trout fishermen and despite the cries of those who felt it would drive away all fishermen the catch-and-release restrictions began to work in Montana as well as in Yellowstone Park. There was a slump in the sale of creels and the catch-and-release sections attracted more anglers than the kill areas.

The "technical" waters of the spring creeks became famous through the writings of a dozen trout gurus and anglers came from afar to fish them—or sometimes to stand and watch other anglers and insist they themselves did not have the techniques needed. The careful fly casters of the East came West and found there were Montana fish insisting upon fine leaders and tiny flies.

At first the visiting fishermen had thought of the West primarily as a place where hardy waders stood in swift, cold water with shifting gravel beneath their waders and threw huge streamers to cannibalistic trout during the fall spawning season for browns—"lochs" if you were a native.

The big streamer chasers are still there, of course, but there is a little of all kinds of fly fishing for trout.

At first, like other tourists, we stared up at the mountains with their stony and snowy peaks and their enormous blankets of evergreens and slide rock. For generations vacationists have gone "to the mountains" and on the way most of them pay little attention to the grasslands or the expanses of ridges and buttes that break up the high plains. At first we looked toward the mountains nearly all of the time and followed the deer and elk at their bases. There were, of course, blue grouse to startle a mountain hunter and there were seldom-seen ruffed grouse along the draws and creeks but we did not hunt them.

We waited for mallards along the open creeks when sudden chills brought the northerners down from Canada and sometimes produced great curtains of steam along the warm spring creeks and brought whispering slush ice down the bigger rivers. We watched and listened when great flocks of musical snow geese milled over lighted towns and sought the mountain passes to the south, thousands of ghost birds in ghost formations that caught the reflections of lights from below. We had squirmed happily in our sleeping bags when night-flying Canadas circled our white tent. But we generally looked toward the mountain ranges.

Then, when we crawled endless distances on our belt buckles after pronghorns we began to realize that there was a wild community on the prairies and in the sage hills, perhaps as interesting as that of the high timber—and perhaps more varied. We began to notice the high grass country and the sage foothills and we looked off toward the Dakotas where Indian history and Indian fable mixed. We saw the rifle pits atop an eastern Montana butte, pits gouged in rocky ground by unknown marksmen and covering all approaches with open lanes of fire from each little trench. And no one could tell us if they were dug by cavalry, feuding ranchers, or hard-pressed cattle thieves. Indian signs cut in the base of the butte were little help.

Some time in the middle sixties we managed to draw our attention from the big ranges and see the gamebirds of the high grasslands and sage country. On my stomach in antelope country I had met a sage cock—drawn up to his full height like a magnified quail, and we had been startled by coveys of Hungarian partridges, little-heralded immigrants simply called "little chickens" by ranchers. There were, of course, the much-sought Chinese pheasants in the river bottoms and coulees—and although we hunted them, their gaudy dress somehow didn't fit the huge landscapes with their sheepherder's monuments and the abandoned mining towns with their cemeteries, stones reminding us bleakly that pioneer children died most frequently in midwinter.

The native sharptail grouse fit the scenes better, prairie and brushland birds that somehow accepted the settlers and their sod plows with the long moldboards. The sharptails accepted the miles of grainfields—better than have the sage grouse who have been driven from their ancestral homes by the huge 8-wheel-drive articulated diesel tractors that turn sage slopes into cropland—progress that worries bird hunters who may not know that the sage itself is a comparatively recent occupant of much of its range. A romantically inclined hunter with a bird dog is likely to feel the baseball-capped tractor jockey does not fit the scene as well as the broad-brimmed horseman now likely to appear only in fall when the herds are moved down from the high pastures.

Pointing dogs lead hunters to ground they might not cover otherwise, teaching them the spots where upland coveys appear year after year, leading the upland gunner to his own personal traditions. When he talks to a landowner he sometimes has the strange feeling of knowing the rancher's land better than the rancher does. I stood, out of breath, on the crest of a rocky ridge yesterday with a hundred square miles of Montana spread before me. It could have been a scene painted by Charles Russell except that I caught the glint of motor traffic miles away on an interstate highway and the contrail of a commercial jet high enough that it escaped the lower wind that tore cumulus clouds into streamlined tatters.

It had been a long time since I first watched a covey of Hungarian partridges sweeping down from that ridge, teetering slightly and reflecting sun from their wings as they set them toward a distant coulee while a big-eyed bird dog watched them in futile fascination. The rancher who had given me permission to hunt there yesterday was the fourth one who had owned the land since we first came to Montana. It is a rather secret place and when I am gone I wonder if another hunter will find it and who the owner will be then.

I know other areas in other states where condominiums and shopping centers have taken over treasured long-time private places and where broad highways have replaced sand roads and trails. In Montana the pace of change is slower and although Charlie Russell deplored the "booster" and trails plowed under, those other years are somehow not so distant.

There was the weathered old .44-40 cartridge case I found beside a natural rifle rest above a canyon used by generations of deer—that cartridge beloved by hunters of human generations long gone. There was the cache of diary notes left by hunters of the 1920s in a natural hiding place in the Crazy Mountains. They had come there for years and the last entry was in 1926 but the canyon must have been much as we found it except for the faraway whine of a chainsaw. And I realize it has been almost thirty years since we found the notes and left them there. I could not find them now.

Love of trout streams, elk ridges, and sage-grouse slopes grows with time. They cannot remain completely unchanged but there are parts of the world where change is slow.

ON THE RIVER OF COLD FIRES

Tim Cahill

The writer considered the weather and felt somehow obliged to issue a challenge to God. He was, apparently, a man who had never read The Book of Job. There were several of us standing waist deep in the icy river, cursing our leaky rubber waders and unloading lunch gear from one of the three rafts. It was one in the afternoon, the warmest part of a cold day, and the rain, which had started earlier that morning, was falling in sheets out of a glacial gray sky. It seemed biblical in proportion, this rain, ridiculously cold, and it drummed down on our heads without surcease, making us both snappy and stupid. The temperature fluttered just above the freezing mark and the downpour was so constant, so unrelenting, that my fingers weren't working well in the cold. I could see them there, fumbling redly at the end of my arms.

"Funny fingers," I thought, stupidly. "Aren't much good."

And then, at that point, the writer said this thing and everyone backed away from him.

I'm not being coy here. I didn't say it. There was another writer along for the trip. Aside from us—two writers—there were a couple of restauranteurs, a musician, a couple of professional fishing guides, and a real estate salesman.

All of us were slowly freezing to death, and no one was mentioning this fact. There were two women on the trip, and none of the men was going to say anything at all about the possibility of our impending icy demise until one of the women at least complained. The women, for their part, had equal and opposite concerns regarding the men. Thanks to the issue of sex, there would be no complaining on this trip.

The writer—this other writer, understand—looked up into the low gray clouds for a moment. A small stream of ice water formed and poured off his nose.

"You know," he said brightly and full of false good cheer, "God's a wimp if this is the worst He can throw at us."

And all of us sort of backed away from the blasphemer. People who had never been to church in their lives made for the bank. It was April, in Montana: there are lots of things that can happen to you in this, the cruelest month, and it doesn't do to tempt fate. I had a sudden vision of Ice Age corpses frozen throughout time in the shimmering belly of some renegade glacier. Shriveled limbs. Open mouths, silent screams. An eternity of ice.

Give you an idea of how miserable it was:

We built a fire at lunch. It took a very long time to catch, longer to flame up in any satisfactory way. It took longer than the hour we had for lunch. I know that because no one got warm at lunch. The Crow Indians say that an Indian builds a small fire and stands close; a white man will build a large fire and stand far away. We were, for the most part, white men and we had built a large fire. But the ground was wet, the wood was wet, and rain kept falling from the sky. We stood very close to the large fire, breathing smoke and waiting for some warmth to develop. "This," a restaurant owner said, "is a cold fire."

"Sounds like a book title," one of the writers said. "On the River of Cold Fires."

"I mean it," the first man said. "You could freeze to death in front of this fire."

That's how cold it was.

The river was peculiar. Once you began, you were committed to a three-day run at the very least. It was all canyon walls and wilderness until the first feasible take-out point, sixty miles downstream. When someone in your party challenges God to make you as miserable as possible, and there are a couple of days left on the trip, and your fingers don't work very well, it takes an act of will to enjoy corrugated canyon walls soaring 500, 800, 1,000 feet overhead.

There was no one else on the river, because anyone who knows it well enough to float knows that late April can be unpleasant. So there were no other human beings in sight. Not for three days. It could have been Alaska. It could have been America before the white man.

The river, in fact, had been named by Lewis and Clark in 1804. They named it for the Secretary of the Navy in that year. It wasn't a big, important presidential river, a Jefferson or a Madison. Just a small Secretary-of-the-Navy-sized river, a little bit of a secret actually, and if I were to mention its name, my companions would discuss the matter with me using baseball bats and two by fours. No matter that the fishing was grotesque and the weather hideous: these folks, Montanans all, believe in the Conservation of Misery.

So, for the purposes of obfuscation, I'll call it the River of Cold Fires.

We had been invited on the trip by a river guide named Jim Kent who works out of Livingston, Montana. His first clients would hit the water toward the end of May and probably avoid any blizzards. Before that, Kent needed to check his gear. Were the rafts leaking; were the tents in good repair; were the grill and griddle working well? It was chancy, setting out on the third week of April. But, what the hell, we'd be lucky. The weather, which had been inching up into the 80s the week before, would surely hold.

There was a black lab along on the rafting trip, the kind of dog that joyously plunges into freezing river water to retrieve fallen ducks on a late fall day. The black lab had the same name as the river, and he lay atop one of the softer mounds of gear strapped into the raft and cried piteously as the cold rain fell. That should suggest some measure of our discomfort. It's cold when you have to find a blanket for a black lab.

We had about six more hours to float after the day's cold lunch and a strong upriver wind drove pellet-hard drops of near-frozen rain into our faces. The rain seeped into our clothes.

It was the worst, the coldest, and the most miserable kind of weather. The temperature hovered near freezing so that the rain wanted to be snow. Soon enough, it started to fall: snowflakes the size of quarters that splashed against the exposed skin of my face.

The fish, after twenty-four hours of cold rain, were hunkering at the bottom of the river, not feeding much, not rising to the occasional hatch of mayflies. To catch trout on a fly rod in these conditions you have to throw weighted nymphs at them. These are big fat heavy flies, difficult to cast, and they go bouncing along the rocks at the bottom of the stream where they supposedly look like the larvae stage of various insects. These insect entrees form 90 percent of a trout's diet.

Nymphing is a frustrating method of fishing, especially from a moving boat, because the fly is floated deep and the only way to tell a strike is by a sudden movement of the line on the surface. And since the fly hits snags or snags on rocks, you often strike at nonexistent fish.

Every twentieth cast or so, your fly catches something on the bottom and stays there. You try to shake it loose a couple of times but nothing happens and so you point the tip of your rod along the bad destiny of your line and just let the $1.95 fly snap off. A gift to the river. Then, in the icy rain, you get to tie another big fat wooly worm to your tippet. With numb, shaking fingers.

Because the water was dark with rain, I was using flies with white rubber legs and bits of silvery tin foil on their underside. Such flies do not imitate any known insect. Their advantage, in high, dark water, is that the fish can see them.

People who fly fish—I've said this before, but it bears repeating—are rather like people who have some strange sexual fetish. "If I can't do it with whips and chains, I'd rather not do it at all." The fly fisherman says, "If I can't catch them on a fly, I'd rather not catch them at all."

Such purists regard bait fishermen as Neanderthals, spin-fishermen as jerks. Some even frown on the use of un-bug-like flies like the ones I was using. I mean it: they actually frown at you.

It was snowing heroically. Great swirls of spring snow were spinning up the river and the flakes had given way, in the depths of the canyon, to hard stinging bits of spring snow, indistinguishable from hail.

I had caught one fish in two days, and it seemed fruitless to flog the water with my outlandish flies and offend the purists at the same time. I sat in the bow of the raft, curled against the cold. The grassy sections of the river banks were bright green. The snow had begun to stick in patches so that the world was the gray of the sky, the brown of the river, and Christmas on the bank.

A herd of mule deer stood on the bank and regarded us with some sarcasm. They stared at the rafts and turned inward for a herd conference: "These are the guys who challenged God to give them bad weather, in April, in Montana," they informed one another. Or so it seemed. A large buck gave the signal: "Let's get out of here," and they turned, springing up toward a break in the canyon wall—twenty-seven of them fleeing from bad luck until all that was visible of them was their white back ends pogoing up the gray of a rocky draw.

There was, I noticed, a snowdrift forming on my lap.

*

God works in mysterious ways. My reading suggests that She hasn't taken personal challenges in regard to weather quite seriously since the days of the Old Testament.

Montana's weather is changeable enough on the natch. Prudent drivers carry survival gear in the trunks of their cars eight months out of the year. A couple of sleeping bags and a bit of food can be lifesavers in a sudden blizzard. On January 20th, 1954, in a mining camp near Montana's continental divide at Rogers Pass, the temperature dropped to 70° below zero, a record low for the lower forty-eight states.

If Montana has the record for bitter cold, it also holds all the records for changeability. On January 23rd, 1916, an arctic outbreak in Browning dropped the temperature from 44° above to 54° below in twenty-four hours. Another American record concerns a warming trend: on January 11, 1980, in Great Falls, Montana, the temperature rose from 32° below to 15° above in less than seven minutes.

More to the point, Montana also enjoys the meteoritical oddity of severe late-spring blizzards. In the area east of Great Falls—our general location—a storm bringing forty-mile-an-hour winds dropped forty-five inches of snow on May 17, 1903. The week before, lilacs had been in bloom and people had been planting their gardens.

Sixty-six years later, On April 24 of 1969, after a week of temperatures in the mid to high 80s, 100-mile-an-hour winds driving freezing snow killed an estimated 100,000 head of livestock. Drifts twenty-five feet high covered spring green grass. Certain towns were blacked out for over a month.

Indeed, according to meteorologists, unusually warm spring temperatures are a harbinger of the dreaded spring blizzard. Warm air can hold great amounts of moisture, and, if a Pacific cold front is approaching—one of those big systems that extends in a long finger from the Gulf of Alaska to California—something nasty is going to happen. As the cold front moves eastward, it pulls warm, moisture-laden air up into Montana from the Gulf of Mexico. When the cold front finally spills over the Rockies, it encounters that ridge of warm, wet air coming up from the South. The cold air swirls, counter-clockwise, creating an intense area of surface low pressure.

All of which means that in late spring, in Montana, it is possible to get a bad sunburn on April 24th and be wading thigh deep through a severe blizzard on the 25th.

The hard, wind-driven pellets of snow had given way again to fat swirling flakes that splashed against the skin like a mother-in-law's kisses. No one was fishing anymore, and those of us who weren't rowing sat still and morose, freezing in stolid stoicism. The drift on my lap was a foot deep. I wore wool socks over my gloves and a triple layer of jackets. I was shivering involuntarily, but almost numb to the cold. It didn't seem to matter much anymore.

One of the other rafts drifted by. I called to the writer, who was rowing. "A wimp, huh?"

He smiled his bright smile, full of false good cheer, and nodded upriver. We were coming into a deep part of the canyon. The storm had brought scads of wildlife down to the River of Cold Fires: there were deer and raccoon on the banks, there were beaver and coyotes. Someone thought he saw a few mountain goats on the lower ridges of the canyon wall. It was hard to tell if the patches of white were goats or small snow drifts. There were fir and pine trees clinging impossibly to tiny niches in the canyon walls. They were all covered with a dusting of snow. Downriver, in the wind tunnel of the canyon, snow was falling in twisted ribbons, dancing toward us in a swirling glacial polka.

It was beautiful, in a savage and entirely unsettling manner. Few people, I knew, were dumb enough to risk the River of Cold Fires in the season of spring blizzards. So the sight belonged to me. It was beautiful and it was mine: the River of Cold Fires in the season of snow. I thought: this is one of those intangible things I'll own forever because I've paid for it, paid for it in equally intangible dues. The idea was wondrous cold comfort. There was a physical sensation that belonged to the idea: some strange combination of cold and inspiration. A rivulet of ice water found its way down my spine and I felt the entire surface of my flesh blossom out into goose bumps.

THE GREAT WHITE TROUT

Alston Chase

My brother Richard sat embedded in our sagging Salvation Army sofa, eyeing me uneasily. Something remained unresolved between us, and we both knew it.

Like our earlier reunions, the critical mass of our personalities created strong undercurrents that threatened to disturb the surface. Richard and his family, visiting from Massachusetts, were on a tour of the West in their station wagon. We were gathered, that September of 1978, in the one-room log cabin near Montana's Smith River that I and my wife Diana and our three boys had built with our own hands six years earlier.

Like many Montanans, Diana and I were refugees. As a college professor at Ohio State University and Macalester College, I had lived through the campus turmoil of the sixties and early seventies. Colleges were going to hell in a handbasket, as they always are. At Macalester, student protests were taking a distinctly ugly turn. The war in Vietnam was ripping the campus apart, severing our last links with Aristotle and Shakespeare. The best and the brightest were holding professors hostage and mau-mauing administrators.

After the Kent State massacre of 1970, Diana and I began to look for a place in Montana; and in 1972 we bought this 3,000-acre ranch overlooking the Smith River's spectacular canyon. I gave up my tenure at Macalester. Diana sold her Queen Anne desk and I my piano and we moved full time to the ranch. We built some cabins and founded a summer environmental program for teenagers. I embarked on a career as a freelance writer.

The ranch, more than fifty miles from the nearest town, had no electricity or telephone. The nearest neighbor was ten miles away. In winter we were snowbound two months at a time. Having no lights we lived by the sun. The rhythm of our days changed with the seasons, our habits forming simple patterns. The solitude was magical and soothing. Nothing over the horizon mattered.

The place was teeming with wildlife—antelope, elk, whitetail and mule deer, mountain lion, lynx, bobcat, bighorn sheep, and, of course, our ubiquitous Montana neighbor, the coyote.

The Smith River flowed through our place below steep limestone cliffs. I developed an intimate acquaintance with the rainbow and brown trout that lived there. I was a fanatical fly fisherman, living in trout heaven.

Indeed, the Smith's trout first lured me to this place and it was Richard who gave me the love of fishing. But now his visit threatened the bucolic serenity that I had found here.

The problem between us started in Yellowstone National Park on July 4, 1947. Our father, an army officer, had just returned from Europe and was moving us, his family, to Fort Lewis, Washington. On our way we stopped at Yellowstone for the first time. We stayed in a cabin at Fishing Bridge. I had never before seen trout so large. Below the bridge big cutthroats moved slowly and insolently around the tangled lines of frenetic fisherman. Richard and I begged our father to take us fishing.

Our father rented us complete and identical outfits—bait-casting rods with snelled flies attached. He drove us to an isolated spot on the Yellowstone where the family picnicked while my brother and I fished.

By lunchtime Richard had caught his limit, including a beautiful sixteen-incher he had coaxed from under the near bank. I had not gotten a strike. I stayed at the river while the family went back to the cabin. By dark I had only caught a slight case of sunstroke.

During the next four days Richard beached his limit each day and I failed to get a strike. On our last day in the park, my parents rented a boat and guide to take me fishing in Yellowstone Lake. Unfortunately, to be fair, they let Richard go along too. My brother and I used identical tackle. I trolled from the port side and he from the starboard. He caught his limit again, of course. I didn't get a nibble.

From then on trout fishing became my obsession. We lived at Fort Lewis for two years and I devoted every spare minute to fishing. At every opportunity I rode my bicycle to one of the nearby trout lakes or to the Nisqually River, fishing until dark. I took a paper route and every cent earned went to fishing tackle. I memorized books by famous fishermen. I devoured outdoor magazines. I tied flies. But I couldn't catch trout.

My brother did none of these things. He played football and drove around Tacoma with his "Tillicum gang" picking up girls. But whenever he deigned to wet a line his success was invariably phenomenal.

My obsession with catching trout was fueled by a deeper anger. Richard, nearly three years older, was bigger and faster than I. He could beat me up, and often did. I feared him. Yet I could not avoid him. My assigned role in childhood was to be his assistant. I played Igor to his Frankenstein.

Richard was forever making model airplanes, or taking toasters apart to see what made them work.

"Hold these pieces of balsa wood together *just like this*," he would say, "until the glue dries."

Then later: "No! You did it all wrong! You've ruined it. I said to hold it like *this*, not like *that*!" Following which I would usually be pummelled.

As we grew older I began to fight back. Our battles became fiercer but less frequent. Going to different schools, we saw less of each other. When we were apart I felt very close to Richard and admired him enormously. But if together long enough we would always, ultimately, fight. It seems we loved each other abstractly, but despised each other concretely.

Trout fishing continued to be a wall that separated us. But one day, in the spring of 1951, in Berchtesgaden, Germany, our competition underwent a strange transformation. Our family was vacationing in this famous alpine resort where Hitler had a summer place—the "crow's nest"—and where he had built bunkers in anticipation of fighting out the last days of the war. Yet little here had changed in the six years since Hitler self-destructed with the rest of Nazidom in Berlin. The village was still intact and the hotel—the Berchtesgardaner Hof—still served meals on linen tablecloths embroidered with swastikas. And while Hitler's house had been bombed out, his old caretaker was there still.

One afternoon my brother and I visited the crow's nest. The caretaker showed us through the labyrinth of bunkers behind the house and we admired the view of the valley and lake below through the huge expanse that once held what must have been the biggest picture window in the Third Reich.

Not daring to go anywhere unarmed, however, I had bought fishing gear along as well. And as we passed the lake on our return to the hotel, I noticed trout rising. We stopped immediately, unpacked our tackle and took stations on the shore where a small stream entered the lake. On the first cast I hooked and landed a one-foot brown trout. When a second trout hit my line, Richard, still without a strike, asked what fly I was using. He began tying the same fly on his leader as I played another trout somewhat larger than the first.

After I had caught and released trout number three, Richard insisted we exchange places. I landed number four while he was untying a knot in his leader. Then he demanded we swap rods. Still, I kept my appointment with trout number five while my brother thrashed the water furiously.

When the sixth trout was beached, Richard insisted we stop. He said nothing on our way back to the hotel and never mentioned the incident.

Richard never went trout fishing again. Now he was here, at my ranch, where it is harder to avoid fishing than it is to keep dry swimming. And I had promised to take Richard, his wife Evi, and their children to the river the next day. I wasn't looking forward to renewing our rivalry, but I had to ask the question.

"Would you like to fish while you're down at the river?" I asked.

"After you outfished me in Berchtesgaden," he answered, breaking twenty-seven years of silence about the incident, "I lost interest in trout fishing. I'd like to spend tomorrow looking for geodes."

His answer did not relieve my apprehension. I wanted to fish myself, but not with my brother as an audience.

The next day we hiked down the steep canyon trail we called "suicide" to the Smith, then up Tenderfoot Creek. We looked unsuccessfully for geodes, but saw a nice black bear near the Tenderfoot. I was the only one to take a rod along. Late in the afternoon, as we were heading back to the buildings, we stopped one more time at the Smith. While Richard's son Ricky was skipping rocks I set up my light Hardy rod and began casting a nymph upstream into the swift riffle where the Tenderfoot merges with the river.

On the second cast I hooked something very large. It took off downstream into a deep pool below a red orange limestone cliff. It halted there, sitting on the bottom and refusing to move. My rod was too limber and leader too slim to allow me to put any pressure on the fish. I asked Richard and Ricky to toss rocks at him. The first toss sent the trout upstream into the heavy current like a flash; then he began a slow drift back into the deep again.

It became a waiting game. I stood straining at the rod while my brother and nephew tormented the animal with rocks. But the fish never seemed to tire. Evi and my nieces got bored with the whole affair and left. The sun disappeared. By now the trout had become so accustomed to rocks raining down on him that nothing would make him budge. A beaver appeared, apparently from nowhere, and insisted on swimming back and forth across my line. Ricky began throwing rocks at the beaver.

It got dark and bats skimmed across the water. Apparently their radar told them my line was some kind of insect, for they began attacking the leader just above the waterline. The entire Animal Kingdom, it seemed, was fighting for the trout. While trying to keep tension on the fish, I moved the line back and forth to dodge the bats.

Richard stood by my side, quietly offering support.

"Don't rush him or you'll lose him."

"Don't put on too much pressure, we've got time."

Five hours after the struggle began, the fish came to the surface, moving to the opposite bank. A half hour later, I dragged a large brown trout into the shallow water at my feet. My brother fell on the fish, straddling it with his knees. As it thrashed, the fly came out of its mouth. Richard reached down its throat and yanked it out of the water by the teeth. He held up the trout, blood pouring from a cut in his hand.

The next day Richard and I drove the 250-mile round trip to Dan Bailey's Fly Shop to have the trout measured for the fisherman's "Wall of Fame." Five pounds fourteen ounces! After we had taken a profile of the fish at Bailey's, we headed back to the ranch.

We didn't talk much on the way back, but I felt very close to my brother. I also felt ashamed at my apprehensions and competitiveness. Richard had outgrown our childhood rivalry, why couldn't I?

Richard and his family left the next day. Three years later Diana and I sold the ranch. We live now near Livingston, where the fishing is wonderful. I still like to cast a line occasionally, but I confess that some of the edge is gone. Had I been looking for something else all along? I don't know. But whatever sated my passion for fishing, I think, had something to do with Richard.

3 GROWING UP

THE GHOST TOWNS OF MY TIME

Bill Stockton

I was born in a homestead shack in central Montana in 1921. It burned down when I was two years old.

After the fire my widowed mother abandoned her 160 acres and, along with her four kids, one milk cow, and a dozen Plymouth Rock hens, moved to town. Her land, like thousands of similar quarter sections, was reclaimed by the government. And I would spend all of my formative years hunting and chasing that damned old milk cow through all the back lots and back alleys of Winnett, Montana.

I return to the homestead site from time to time. Where I used to play as a baby, cows now lumber by, and herds of antelope graze among pieces of glass, old buttons, and dried harness straps. On my last trip I salvaged from the caved-in cellar my parents' bedstead. Roots!

Most of the homesteads in the semi-arid regions of the West were too small to maintain a family—at least at the grain and livestock prices of those days. The politicians who had written the Homestead Act had assumed, for their convenience and to the disaster of the farm, that 160 acres out west was equivalent to 160 acres in Iowa. Instead, if they had established individual homesteads of 320, 480, and 640 acres, depending on the terrain, and at the same time had set a floor on the price of agricultural products, the face of the countryside would be much different today.

Of course, the government with the Homestead Act had accomplished its purpose: it had settled the West, it had subsidized the banks, the railroads, and the implement dealers, and it had eased certain urban centers of its unemployed. Then in the thirties and forties the government would reverse itself and redistribute the homesteads to the large ranchers in the form of locally controlled grazing districts. The depopulation of the countryside, which had begun in the twenties, would continue to the present day. The migration of people was in reverse.

I returned to the land in 1950. The little towns that had sprung up as service centers for the homesteaders were still there but half empty. In the decades to follow a few of them would survive on a diminished scale—others, without rural people to support them, would all but vanish. Some of these towns had been laid out with great optimism for the future and in a grandiose style; others had just happened along old cow trails. But now they all had the same look—something that could have been.

The bank had been the first to pull out—of course. It was followed by the grocery, implement lot, railroad, and school. The banker joined the urban crowd and aided the politician, economist, and sociologist to manipulate and contrive the present "cheap food" policy. This policy, not the technological revolution, whereby a way of life should be sacrificed in lieu of the profit-efficiency panacea, would be the demise of rural America and the small town.

Very often young city people express to me a desire to return to the land. "No way," I tell them. "Corporate capitalism is not interested in a free-enterprise way of life for you. They prefer to hand you food stamps and congest you in a filthy, urban ghetto.

"In my day I was aware of the exodus of millions of rural people from the countryside—I doubt if the direction will ever be reversed. Hell, 2,000 American farmers and ranchers went bankrupt last week. Thirty-five years ago grain and livestock prices were 90 percent of parity—today, they are 50 percent of parity. You can make a better living on welfare. Throughout history the people who raise food—the peasants, the clod-hoppers, the *cul terreux,* as the French call them ("dirt asses" in

English) have never counted for much—they're the scapegoats for almost everything. Remember, the French royalty used to quarter them. Even now, every time the peasants try to revolt the hired goons are there, to murder them if necessary. If you don't believe me, travel to Central America and witness the slaughter first hand."

A MATTER OF BLOOD

Scott Hibbard

On Tuesday, July 13, 1976, Henry Sieben Hibbard was killed in his Piper Super Cub while looking for bulls. A seventeen-year-old cowboy died with him. A General's aide in World War II, graduate of Harvard Business School, ten-year State Legislator, and candidate for the United States Senate in 1972, this prominent third-generation rancher was dead at fifty-six, killed on his own ranch. I was in London that day thinking how wonderful it was to not have a care in the world as I watched the changing of the Queen's Royal Guard. Twenty-four hours later I was at the ranch, thirty miles south of Cascade, Montana.

An aging, half-breed cowboy called to offer his condolences, one who had taught me much of what I know about the art of working cattle on horseback. "A damned ol' bull," he said.

The following year, Charlie Hodson, king pin of the neighboring Hodson Ranch and wild-horse wrangler in the 1930s, threw his left hand up to fend off a fallen powerline he saw at the last second while gathering bulls on horseback. His foreman, Joe Enger, was riding with him. Charlie's horse died instantly and Charlie was dead too, Joe said. Bubbles were coming out of his mouth when Joe left to get help. There was no pulse.

When Joe Enger returned with the neighbor, Charlie was uncinching the saddle from his dead horse. He would lose his left arm. He would spend sixty-five days in a Dallas burn center but would recover well enough to ride again prior to his fatal heart attack thirteen months later.

This cattle ranching seems to require a certain amount of human blood. Take flesh from the land and the land takes flesh in return. Sometimes we're granted reprieve. Like the spring that comes every year, sometimes when all is thought lost life is given back, like forgiven debt. The issue here is currency. With a bank it's money. With ranching it's flesh, as though balloon payments made to retire a mortgage. For what, one may ask, is this debt incurred?

Whatever it is has something to do with the communion of people with land, working in unison, for mutual benefit, where land is shaped by people and people by land. A cause essentially of heart where one's reward is primarily in the doing of the work, and tangible accomplishment. Ranching is not particularly profitable. Historically, for most ranchers the business is doing well if it makes money six years out of ten. Hence the importance of heart. Like religion, or love, it teaches us that material goods are not one's only measure of wealth.

In time the ranch becomes an expression of the rancher, as children do their parents. We don't, of course, control our children nor do we control the land. At best we help our children, as we do the land, to be the best they can be. And ultimately the parent becomes an expression of the child, and the rancher an expression of the ranch. As the land is basic, physical, fundamental, tough, compassionate, nurturing, and sometimes cruel, so are we. And as the land is a living entity it must be worked with rather than worked on. It requires a melding of human effort with the land's natural propensity to grow things. Therein lies the art.

Ranchers are kicked by cows, thrown on the ground by horses. We get fingers caught in machinery. Sometimes people are killed. Yet we persevere, as though fighting for a cause or waiting for the rewards of endurance, like a winter of calf-killing cold followed by a growing season with the right moisture at the right times.

The land feeds us and, to varying degrees, we feed it. The rancher may feel that he is giving much more than he is taking, feeding more of himself to the ranch than the ranch feeds back. The rancher may feel forsaken, in the sense of living for a cause of heart and losing his heart in the process. This is particularly true for those who have lost their all in order to feed their creditors. Often the rancher's identity is the ranch. When the ranch is lost so is he. The temptation may be to put the .357 to one's forehead and let one's thumb do a tap dance on the trigger. Some do. Sometimes, it seems, we indeed are forsaken. A leap of faith may be in order. Hope, my father would say, springs eternal.

In ranching all is seasonal. Each season demands certain activities, and as one season follows another so does the routine that goes with it. Faces change, machinery changes, new practices are introduced and others refined, but in essence the work remains the same: basic and straightforward, like pushing cattle through a chute or baling hay, repeating familiar motions until the task is complete. The rancher learns to tolerate boredom. He becomes a creature of routine. Though there is challenge in ranch work, and though the work at best is interesting, it lacks stimulation. You become, essentially, a laborer with a view.

In time, for those of an intellectual bent, a certain malaise sets in. After a point one simply stops growing. It has to do with starvation of imagination. Like the field that hasn't been farmed in decades, some become sodbound. As does the field, the rancher needs periodic cultivation if he is to continue growing. If not he may find his intellectual skills becoming clumsy, like a violinist turned carpenter who, in returning to the violin, finds his fingers too muscled to play with dexterity.

Most people have an inherent need to grow. In ranching, as with most businesses, it starts with learning the necessary skills, then if one is born or married into or wealthy enough to purchase a ranch it progresses to the administration of the ranch as a business. At this point other skills are required. One must deal with bankers, lawyers, accountants, insurance agents, bureaucrats, legislators. One is again on a fairly steep learning curve and, like all curves, in time it levels out. When it does one must look beyond the ranch to civic or ranch-related organizations and boards if one wishes to continue growing in the industry. Some look for new ideas to restructure grazing and farming practices, or employee management.

But for most, when it is time to grow there is nothing to which one can grow. Five years is a long time for most ranch employees to remain with the ranch. Married couples stay longer, but beyond a point only if they are willing to live with stasis. Either they reach the extent of their abilities or they're happy with their level of activity or they look for a better position elsewhere with more responsibility and higher pay. In many cases, when one can no longer grow in one's occupation, one switches occupations, and in the case of ranching often to those less physically demanding and more financially promising. The monetary rewards ranching can offer are more limited than many business enterprises. As a result, the ranching industry continually loses some of its best people. Those who stay most often do so because they love it.

Ranching has no corporate ladder. That is part of its great allure and one of its problems. The rancher who is owner-operator at age twenty-five will be doing essentially the same things for the same pay at age seventy-five. Economically speaking, the best for which most ranchers can hope are those few good years, those with prosperous growing seasons and relatively high commodity prices. For change and challenge he must look beyond the ranch.

Three friends immediately come to mind in Helena, all of whom are on a career path, one a public employee, one with an out-of-state corporation, one a small business owner. Within the past six months all have moved to higher paying jobs with more responsibility in other cities. What they have is career opportunity. What ranchers have is place, and, important though it is, one can't live for place alone and sometimes ranching will ask that. After a point, to find challenge and growth one must look beyond place, but hopefully in a manner that will enrich rather than erode the rancher's connection to his place.

In essence, the enterprise insists that you become basic. There is little room for dreamers in a business whose nucleus is the physical world. One thinks in physical terms, like cows, tractors, weather. Management is a process of logistical planning: buying pipes in the spring to repair water lines so you can irrigate in order to have enough hay to feed the cows in the winter.

One must also all too often work seven-day weeks, months on end. Feeding and calving are followed by farming and irrigating, which is followed by haying, all of which can be relentless masters. There is always something that needs doing, now. You live at your place of work. Your home is your office and office hours are whenever you're home, as witnessed by telephone calls at 10:00 P.M. or hunters knocking before daylight. Perhaps one of ranching's greatest lessons is in the persistence it requires, and among its greatest gifts the toughness imbued in body and heart, the physical and emotional stamina one learns, the compassion the animals teach, and the self-reliance it engenders when something has to be done and there is no one else to do it.

But, like my grandmother used to say, you earn everything you get in this world. In this case the price paid has something to do with living in paradise yet being unable to see the view. Inevitably the view gets cluttered with the problems at hand, which, perhaps more often than they should, seem insurmountable. We are at the whim of too many forces beyond our control, like the anchovie harvest off the coast of Argentina that once had a direct bearing on the cost of feeding cattle (anchovies were a feed ingredient), which affected how much feeders could pay ranchers for their calves.

The land can be a beautiful yet cruel master, like God, it seems, and indeed it is like a God to us. There is something of a love-hate relationship at work here and it has to do in part with the issue of control. Who is master, the man or the land? All too often, it seems, it's the latter. We do what the land and livestock demand of us when it's demanded, and perhaps a little too often, more is asked for than we can deliver. It's an imposition some come to hate.

Some see their lives ground up by endless, mindless detail. Things always need fixing. We focus on immediate, minor concerns and lose sight of why we are here, the spiritual wholeness, the intrinsic goodness inherent in nurturing living, growing things (particularly, it seems, when one doesn't get rich doing so). The reward of the work is that one can point to what he's done as though a tangible expression of who and what he is, like a freshly plowed field or a newly constructed corral. The work is real, you can touch it, your kids can see it, and it can be appreciated by almost anyone.

The rancher can be seen as the caretaker of open space and the wildlife habitat that goes with it. He can be seen as one who is preserving some of what is the best of this nation. He has the satisfaction of seeing life cycles complete and repeat themselves, and of complementing those cycles. Some ranchers can think it is indeed an honor to do the work.

It is easy to get caught up in our own little kingdoms, thinking the world ends at our boundary fence. It becomes easy to forget the outside world except for brief excursions to town for parts and groceries. The problem is the world doesn't end at your fenceline, as witnessed by the distant mountain snowpack that feeds your streams or the roads that help spread noxious weeds. The temptation may be to stay in one's own world, but in so doing the world forgets you. Life can pass you by. That's O.K. until you find out that a lot of things happen out there that have bearing on what you do, how you do it, and to what degree you are king in your own kingdom. We are not as independent as we often think we are, and after a while one learns that.

Nonetheless, to a degree the kingdom remains, and in a sense this is most evident in the family. In its most constructive sense, the ranch becomes a vehicle for family unity in work and in play, as the family becomes the vehicle for the wholesome growth of the land itself. The kids grow up understanding and learning what Mom and Dad do. Skills are passed on. Common sense is learned, as is responsibility in the caring of animals, plants, equipment. Values are instilled that are seemingly becoming much less common in modern-day life. Family ranches embody what has traditionally been the backbone of this country, and as their numbers dwindle they are becoming more like national treasures, reminders of who we've been and, perhaps, to what we would like to return.

At its best the family ranch is a tool to achieve family love and cooperation for the mutual benefit and growth of the individuals and land involved. At its worst it becomes a vehicle of greed, pitting family member against family member in the struggle for control. Noninterested family members may force the sale of the ranch so they can get their money out of it. Bitterness deepens, the ranch is lost and the family broken up. Perhaps the problem with family ranches is family, that it would be a backhanded blessing if the family had only one heir. Succession would be clear. There would be little room for family squabbling.

Yet the more heirs there are the more the family is forced into cooperation, and into dealing with family relationships and personal goals in a spirit of mutual respect and trust. The business is there to serve the family, but only if the family serves the business, like the old adage among sheepmen: you take care of the sheep, they'll take care of you. As such, each member realizes he is an important part of a whole, and not *the* whole. Therein lies the strength of the family.

The nucleus of family is part of what gives ranching its special identity, an identity which becomes more special as the numbers of ranches and ranch families decline. This is particularly true where generations of family history are involved. By some universal law, it seems, the longer a ranch is held in the family, the harder it is to keep. If you're a rancher you're somebody, particularly if the ranch has been in the family for some generations. But ranchers are not elitists. They work with their hands. They have manure on their boots. Yet in the eyes of many they warrant distinction because they have something a lot of people would like to have, like the chance to ride horses and work cattle, to be their own boss on their own place, and to be keeper of the legendary West.

Not all people, of course, share the rancher's perception of his relationship to the land and its animals. Some argue that ranchers disrupt the wildness and the inherent freedom of the land. But it can also be argued that the rancher is a vehicle by which the land is released from its bondage. With sound grazing and farming practices the rancher is, in fact, helping the land to be its most productive. Like a coach who brings out his athletes' best, the rancher allows the land to meet certain standards of performance, to be the best it can be. Like woodworkers turning timber into furniture, or a school bright students into doctors, or an artist clay into sculpture, the rancher can be the means by which the talent the land has is tapped.

In most cases the rancher's bond to the land is different from that of the backpacker who insists on going unarmed into grizzly country. Most ranchers try to minimize the vagaries of nature, whether through technology or sophisticated grazing methods. We irrigate to minimize drought. We spray knapweed to prevent its usurpation of native grasses. Hiking in grizzly country with one's safety entrusted to the jingle bells around one's neck is not unlike farming without water.

Yet there is wisdom in the backpacker's approach. Dissipate the energy of your attacker by offering no resistance. Better to roll with the punch, the argument goes, than to get knocked down. Better yet, turn his energy against him. That proves difficult with certain bears, but in the case of grasshoppers threatening alfalfa fields, harvest the hoppers with chickens. Then harvest the chickens. Likewise, control knapweed with the livestock you already have rather than with chemicals. There is room for alternative thought in ranching. After all, people do what works and no one has a monopoly on ideas.

For the moment and for the sake of argument, let's remove the rancher from the ranch. Let's say that our society no longer wants domestic red meat, or wild red meat for that matter, and that our nation's food requirements are adequately met from the sea, truck gardens, and imports, and that it's inhumane to ride horses. Let's say that the economic adjustments are made, and that we are redefined as a people in the final transition from an agrarian to a high-tech, urban economy. What then happens to the ranch?

As a society we would still want some ranchland retained as testimony to what was uniquely American. To some extent the resource would be conserved. The enterprise and the people responsible for the enterprise would not. As such, the remaining "ranches" would become shadows of their former selves, like Harriman State Park on the Henry's Fork in Idaho, or the William Randolph Hearst estate at San Simeon, California, places we go to see what we once were, although what we now see is a shell. The life that made it is dead. Its substance is gone. And we will never be able to understand it fully.

Perhaps the Park Service would maintain and operate a big, beautiful, productive ranch much like Williamsburg, Virginia, where we see actors living as we envision our founders to have lived in this nation's infancy. It would be named "The Ponderosa." At best we could see it. We could not participate in it, or know the people involved, how they behave, how they think. We would see a rendition of what we were. We wouldn't see *what* we were.

I think we will never come to this point. People will always have to eat and most people like hamburgers and an occasional steak too well to give them up entirely. There are vast reaches of the West that can be used for little else. There will always, I expect, be people who one way or another will find ways to be ranchers.

In a societal sense, ranching is important lest we forget that we too live in the physical, natural world, that drought means more than higher water bills or brown fairways on the golf course. That not only can an individual function with skill and intelligence in the world of urban professionals, but that he can also have the physical and emotional stamina necessary to endure ranch work. That man may never rule nature, but that he can accentuate its benevolence and minimize its adversity. That one can be an important and integral part in something that will out-live him, something that is greater than he is. That ultimately man is steward to the natural world, that not only does this land and these animals nurture man, but man nurtures them. That not only is land useful in providing food by efficient means, it is sacred in its spiritual essence of birth, death and rebirth in the cyclical manner of raising crops and livestock, and generations of families, and in the human blood given in return. That the family should indeed be kept on the land as gatekeepers to the basic American values which serve as the benchmark against which changing societal values are judged. That the private steward is necessary to save the hunter and fisherman from themselves.

Whatever the argument may be, the fact remains that the ranch and the rancher are inseparable from the American character and imagination, and will always be so regardless of the economic longevity of the enterprise. The ranch and the rancher will remain in some fashion because the American people, and very likely the people of the world, would not have it otherwise.

THAT GREAT FALLS YEAR

Wallace Stegner

When my family came down out of Saskatchewan to Great Falls Montana in the fall of 1920 I was eleven years old. For most of my conscious life I had known only our scruffy little village in the valley of the Whitemud River, a village five years younger than I was, and in the summers a homestead as lost out on the prairie as a rowboat in an empty ocean.

I had always been sickly, with croups and coughs and pneumonias, and in winter lived on Scott's Emulsion, a repulsive form of cod liver oil. But I had also lived a life so free and unsupervised that it astonishes me now to remember it. I was much outdoors, both summer and winter. I had owned and used guns since the age of seven or eight, and like frontier boys in general I had grown up killing things—gophers, rabbits, small fur-bearers, even the occasional feral cat whose pelt was worth fifty cents in the St. Louis fur market. And I had secrets darker than I would ever have turned loose. My father's erratic and sometimes unlawful activities had taught me to keep my mouth shut, and given me, along with some private shame, a wariness older than my years. In other ways I was younger, even infantile. And I was studious, a reader, in love with words. When under strain, or when things weren't going well, I sometimes reverted to baby talk that drove my father crazy.

In short, an uncouth sensitive little savage with terminal sniffles, a crybaby with an extensive history of dealing death, a pint-sized loner with big daydreams, clammy self-doubts, and an ego out of proportion to the rest of him.

And ignorant—utterly, wonderfully ignorant. I knew nothing of the world outside my own experience except what I had picked up from books and from the Sears Roebuck and T. Eaton catalogs, and none of that was real. It belonged to the world of school, which was as different from my daily life as summer is from winter. What I remember from school is mainly the poetry we read—Tennyson, Longfellow, Joaquin Miller, Tom Moore. I can turn them on yet, hundreds of lines, like indelible neon in my head. But what I remember from recess is something else: fist fights (daily, but not involving me because I was too little and too timid), and times when the whole unlicked horde of us ran yelling along the cutbank trying to stone to death some unlucky muskrat that had set off upriver with a shining stick of water in his teeth.

Briefly, at the age of three, I had lived in Seattle, and before that in North Dakota and Iowa, and so the outside world must have left some marks on me, but at eleven I retained none of that experience. When our green Essex pulled up in front of our rented house in Great Falls, I was as green as the car, incomparably uninstructed in the arts of civilization, as vulnerable to amazement, wonder, perplexity, apprehension, and delight as if I had been a fifteenth-century Carib brought from his island to the court of Castile.

The court of Castile could not have impressed a Carib any more than our new house impressed me. Though in the year that I lived there I came to know Great Falls pretty intimately; from the Giant Spring to Third Island and from Little Chicago to Black Eagle Park, it was not the big city with its paved streets and streetcars, but the household details that impressed me first. I knew about a lot of these details from pictures in the mail-order catalogs, but, like the places and events of books, they were insubstantial, things heard-about, never seen. Seeing them, experiencing them, was a series of cultural shocks.

Lawns, for instance, those marvelous green naps so lovely to roll on, so cool to bare feet, so sweet-smelling when just mown. I associate them still with Charlie Russell, who lived near us and whose lawn I mowed a couple of times, that summer or the next. But when we arrived, I had never seen a lawn, or imagined one. Front yards in my experience had been weeds and bare dirt and perhaps some dead nasturtiums clinging to strings against the house. On the farm the yard had been an alkali flat. As for back yards, which here seemed to have laundry lines and fruit trees and garden patches, in Saskatchewan they had been littered with bones, kindling piles, feathers, and sometimes, near the chopping block, chicken heads. Here, the miracle of turf impressed me for the first time with the sheer *comfort* of the earth.

Up the middle of our front lawn, like the part in a bartender's hair, a cement sidewalk ran from street to porch steps. I had never seen a sidewalk, either, except the plank ones that had made passable one block on each side of Main Street. I could imagine how clean this would be on muddy days, how easily shoveled in winter, how much of an improvement on our village paths, muddy or dusty depending on the weather, and in winter only trampled troughs through the snow.

On the riser of the top porch step were brass numbers—448 as I remember. They meant that our address, ours alone, recognizable to postman, milkman, iceman, or anyone, was 448 Fourth Avenue North. I had never known anybody with a street address (or, for that matter, a postman, milkman, or iceman). Those numbers promoted me into heightened identity in the midst of all the strangeness, and it was not until I saw that other houses up and down the street had them too that I lost my awe at our new status. But how *ingenious!* said my respectful mind to me. How orderly! How right!

On every side, at every moment, I found household marvels. Electric lights came on at the flip of a switch. No more trimming of wicks and wiping out of smoked lamp chimneys with crumpled newspapers. No more carrying of an inadequate glow from room to room. (But no more tranced moments of staring into a cross in the lamp chimney, either, and wondering who was going to die. Modern technology ignored the omens of folklore.)

The living and dining room in our Great Falls house had hardwood floors whose smoothness absolutely delighted me, and whose unfaded rectangles where other people's rugs had lain spoke of mysterious unknown lives. Until my mother spoiled the floors with our own rugs, I spent a lot of time skating around in my stocking feet in a state of Byzantine exaltation, imagining that I had been transported into an enchanted place and liberated from gravity and friction into a condition known only to birds and fishes.

Before my translation to the advanced civilization of Montana, I had never taken a bath except in a tin washtub in front of the kitchen range, in water warmed on the stove. I was the youngest in the family, and our water came the hard way, by bucket and grunt, up a cutbank from the river and across fifty yards of rough ground, so that I generally got my bath in water that had already cleansed somebody else. But here, in a little room upstairs, were all the things I had seen pictured in the catalogs but had never seen in the porcelain.

Here was a claw-footed long tub into which water poured lavishly, hot or cold, at a turn of a tap. It didn't have to be carried out and dumped later, either, but ran swirling down a hole when you pulled the rubber stopper.

Here was a washbowl, white and gleaming and serviced by similar hot and cold taps. No more tin washbasin on a stand by the kitchen door, no more slop bucket behind a curtain underneath.

And here was the real thriller, a water closet, something I had speculated about, wondering how it worked. It turned out that it was a sort of chair or chamberpot half full of water, that accepted bodily wastes as a chamberpot would, but then at the yank of a chain gulped them down and vanished them. It made the old privy, smelly and fly-blown in summer, icy in winter, with no amenities except an out-of-date Sears Roebuck catalog, so primitive and incompetent in retrospect that I could hardly believe how we had lived only days before.

I was not so dumb that, like Steinbeck's Okies, I thought I had broken the thing the first time I pulled the chain and all that water came down, but I did have to practice on it some to discover that it would not repeat its act at once, that you had to wait a few minutes for it to renew itself before it would gush again. And it did take me a couple of visits before I found that it had a little folding saddle, and did not have to be ridden bareback.

Marvels, sybaritic comforts that within a day I could not have done without. They so fascinated me that for several days I hardly ventured out into the strange streets of town, but contented myself with exploring and experimenting with what I found in the house. I got my monkey fingers into everything, and shortly I got a monkey's come-uppance.

In the baseboard of the living room there were little brass sockets with two holes in them into which could be plugged the cords of lamps. One of these had had its insides unscrewed, leaving a hole about an inch deep and as big around as a quarter. It struck me as a fine secret place to keep my little hoard of nickels and pennies, for it had a brass cover that closed down over it, sealing it away from other eyes. When no one was around, I opened the little door and shoved some coins in against the back wall of the hole.

The world exploded in my face, paralysis flashed through me, I was knocked silly. When I got myself together I felt as if all my hair had been singed off. There was a smell of brimstone. My coins, dented and scorched, were scattered across the floor. Shocked and shamed, but not as ignorant as I had been a minute before, I gathered them up and sneaked away.

It may be that all that episode taught me was not to put fingers or coins into hot electric outlets. But I think it taught me a somewhat larger truth too: nothing potent and attractive is without danger. Civilization is built of thunderbolts.

Shortly I learned some more lessons.

We had arrived so close to the beginning of school, and my mother had been so busy getting us settled, that Sunday came upon us before she could get me down to Strain's Department Store for some new school clothes. Apologetic at having failed me, she wondered if, just for the first day or so, I would mind going in what I had.

I had no problem with that: I think I *wanted* to go in what I had worn up in Canada, for I could see how different Montana was, and it seemed to me that in my Canadian clothes I might look foreign, exotic, and interesting, a hardy frontiersman. And I was not afraid of starting school in a strange place: I looked forward to the opportunity. School was where I shone. In our village I had been the bright boy, had skipped the third grade, and had a letter from my old teacher to my new ones saying that I should be allowed to skip the seventh too, that I was ready for eighth-grade work.

On Monday morning my mother put my brown bag of lunch into my hand and looked me over uncertainly. "Can you do it all right? Would you like me to go with you?"

Have my mother lead me by the *hand* to the *eighth grade?* "Heck no!"

"Have you got your letter?"

I patted my buttoned-down hip pocket.

"Miss Merryman said take it to the principal."

"Sure, sure."

"All right." She stood looking at me a minute, stooped to give me a hug. Her eyes were shiny and her voice a little shaky. "Do well, now. Have a good time. Learn a lot. Come right home after. I'll want to hear all about it."

I can see that little runt setting off down the street, and I want to call him back. My imagination, operating from a base nearly seventy years later in time, cringes. The story-teller in me sees this as the beginning of an Ugly Duckling story, and the Ugly Duckling story requires multiple humiliations before it reaches its triumphant fairy-tale ending in the beauty of white feathers.

Come back, I want to advise him. Put it off a day. Wait until your mother can get you some shoes, at least. Those elkhide moccasins were O.K. for a jerk town on the Whitemud, but they look pretty funny on pavement, in combination with short pants and long black stockings.

While she's at it, have her get you something besides that orange sweater with the turtleneck up under your ears, and the white stripe around the chest that makes you look like a Hampshire shoat. And for God's sake quit stalking pigeon-toed as if you were a six-foot-three Daniel Boone on the track of a bear. Come on back home. Tell your mother you have a headache.

Futile, of course. He left sixty-seven years ago.

On the way to school, if I found myself catching up with other kids, I walked slower. If any showed signs of catching up with me, I walked faster. If confrontations and meetings looked inevitable, I crossed over and walked on the other side of the street. I elected to be remote, mysterious, interesting, aloof, and self-sufficient like Lassiter in *Riders of the Purple Sage*. I regretted that I had had to sell my .22 before we left Canada: it would have completed my character and costume.

Cocooned in self-consciousness and fantasy, I walked through the stares of kids crowding the lawn and the front doors of the junior high school. I found the principal's office. By a girl whose eyebrows went up in astonished circumflexes, I was told to wait. I waited. Eventually I was called.

The principal, a tall lady with braids around her head and glasses on a black ribbon pinned to her breast, put on her glasses and looked across her desk at me. She seemed inclined to smile. She had big teeth.

"Well! What's your problem?"

I dug my letter out of my hip pocket and handed it over. She took off her glasses to read it. Then she put them on to read me. She said, "How old are you, Wallace?"

"Eleven." My squeaky voice made eleven sound so inadequate that I hurried to add, "I'll be twelve in February."

She was already shaking her head. "And you think you belong in the eighth grade?"

"Miss Merryman said I should."

"I know. She says very nice things about you. But do you know how old most eighth graders are? Thirteen or fourteen."

"I've always been the youngest!"

"I expect you have. But that may not have been the best for you. I don't believe in pushing pupils, even very bright pupils as I'm sure you are, so far ahead. Even in Grade Seven, which is where I think you belong, you'll be younger than everyone else."

I had not been prepared for any such rejection. Catastrophic tears rushed to my eyes, my woe bubbled up and overflowed. "Oh, come," the principal said. "If you're big enough to think you belong in the eighth grade you're big enough not to cry over a little disappointment."

Obviously I was not too big to cry. Obviously it was not a little disappointment. Crushed, ashamed, and accusing, I smeared a wrist across my wet eyes, looking as lugubrious and wronged as I knew how. For though I could not help bawling, and hated myself for my weakness, I hoped to gain something by it. Stubbornness plus tears were a formula that had worked for me before, and something told me this principal with the Teddy Roosevelt teeth was a softy like my mother.

She said, almost coaxingly, "You wouldn't want to be placed too high and have to go back. You wouldn't want to fail."

"I won't fail!"

With my letter in her hand, she stood up. She came around the desk. For the first time she got a full view of me, all four feet ten of me, in my Hampshire-shoat sweater and my elk-hide moccasins. "Well, my goodness!" she said. "Aren't you something!" She snorted something like a laugh. She studied me with her knuckles against her teeth. "You really think you can do it, don't you?"

"I know I can," I said, and bravely checked my tears, watching her for the final weakening.

It came. "Oh, why not?" she said suddenly. She leaned and wrote something on a piece of paper and folded the paper into the envelope with Miss Merryman's letter. But she still did not put it in my hands. "You understand that if you can't do it, you'll have to be set back a grade."

"Yes, ma'am. I can do it."

Shaking her head, shrugging, surprised at herself, she handed me the envelope. "Take this to Miss Temby, third room up the hall on the right. That will be your home room."

I felt her hand on the top of my head, my neck was twisted back and forth as if it were threaded and she was trying to start it straight. I looked up into her toothy smile, which at once became a laugh. "Now get," she said. "You're already late, and Miss Temby hates tardiness." A bell rang. I got.

Shaken, relieved, and triumphant, I scuttled into the hall and down it past two rooms crowded with students. I was saying over to myself the name, Miss Temby, so that I wouldn't forget it. I suppose I had visions of conning Miss Temby as I had conned the principal.

I found out, that morning and later, that there were plenty of things besides tardiness that Miss Temby hated, and that she was about as easy to con as the Angel Gabriel. She hated tardiness mainly for the interruptions it caused, but also for the character flaw it revealed. She hated interruptions of all kinds, and character flaws of all kinds. She hated breaches of order and discipline and those who created them. She hated carelessness, forgetfulness, playfulness, and inattention, which she lumped together as signs of irresponsibility. Years later, in troubled sleep, I have seen Miss Temby bending over me stiff with indignation, her eyes like burning coals, and heard through the fading mists of the dream her hissing voice: "Irre*sponsi*ble, Wallace!"

Two things Miss Temby liked, absolute attention and the right answer, and she could speak grudging approval when she got them. But the only thing she ever outright praised was perfection, and that was rare. It was certainly not what I suggested when I stood in her doorway, tardy, delinquent, and clearly lost.

"What room are you looking for?"

"Is this Miss Temby's room?"

"Yes, but I can tell you it's not yours. What grade are you in? Fifth? Sixth? They're in the other wing."

"The principal sent me here. I'm supposed to be in the eighth grade."

Laughter puffed out of the watching class. It hit me in the face like a wind. I don't know if I saw myself then as they saw me, but I do now: a scrawny runt in a sweater that engulfs his ears, his skinny legs in black stockings, his feet in stained moccasins. It is too bad I came before Disney. I held up my letter as proof that I was what I said I was. Miss Temby knocked twice on her desk to silence the laughter, and motioned me in. I stood before her, before them all, with my ears in flames while she read Miss Merryman's letter and the principal's note.

Long pause. Exasperated sigh. Tightened lips. "Good Lord," Miss Temby said. "What next? Well, put your lunch in the cloak room—we don't allow them in desks. While you're at it, leave that sweater in there too. It's a provocation."

More laughter. This time Miss Temby did not silence it by knocking on her desk. Though I could not then have formulated the lesson I was learning, which was that autocrats find scapegoats necessary as lightning-rods to divert away from themselves the hostility their autocracy inspires, I understood with cold clarity that Miss Temby had deliberately humiliated me and invited the class to join her in laughing at me. Hating her, I found a place for my lunch. Hating her, I tore off the hateful sweater that I had myself picked out of the T. Eaton catalog the Christmas before. Hating them all, I slunk back in and found an empty desk, where I sat through an hour of roll call, study cards, and textbook distribution, feeling the eyes slanted at me, the appraising looks, the incredulous smiles. There was not a pupil there, even among the girls, that I would have dared challenge. The boy behind me was as big as a man, and could have used a shave. What I could not deal with physically I dealt with in words, and those unuttered.

Yeah, laugh. Go on, laugh. You're so big, did any of you ever win a prize for killing more gophers than any kid in Saskatchewan? Did any of you ever shoot yourself through the big toe with a .22 long? How many muskrats did you trap last winter, hey? I got fourteen. How many ermines? I got two. How many mink? I got one. And I shot a beaver but he sank and I didn't get him.

How much did you make last winter, trapping? I made eighty dollars. Go ahead, laugh. You'll find out. You'll find out I'm smarter than you, too.

Careful, I want to tell him as he seethes and shrinks and tries to hide his moccasins among the iron legs of his desk and tries to fix his face so that it will register alertness to Miss Temby and aloof indifference to the kids around him. Careful. Because I remember, as he cannot yet know, that in a moment Miss Temby will announce a review test in algebra, to see how much of last year's work has lasted over the summer. And I know, and so does he, that he never heard of algebra. I know that by the frantic exercise of guesswork and common sense he will get a grade of 12 out of a possible hundred, and that Miss Temby the rest of the morning will look at him every now and then with gloomy implacable eyes.

By the time Miss Temby had whipped through our algebra quizzes and announced that most of us had retained nothing, *nothing*, and that we would have to have two weeks of review before we could go on to geometry, it was noon. The bell rang, the pupils swarmed out. I did not. Miss Temby, locking her desk, said to me, "Go outside and get some fresh air. Don't eat your lunch at your desk." My soul said to her, in bitterness, I know more about fresh air than you'll ever know. I'm from *Saskatchewan*. But when I went into the cloakroom to get my lunch, intending to eat it in the hall, both my lunch and my sweater were gone.

I knew what would happen if I went outside. Some kid would be strutting around in my sweater, with the turtleneck up to his eyes, groping blindly, saying, "Where's the eighth grade? I belong in Miss Temby's room." Some other kid would ask if I'd lost my lunch, and produce it, and pretend to hand it to me, and at the last minute pass it over my head to somebody else. Then we would have a nice game of keep-away. The hell with it. I sat gloomily at my desk the whole noon hour.

Somehow I survived that first day. I even, before the year was out, managed to get Miss Temby's grudging approval on several occasions, and at least twice her enthusiastic praise: once when she asked us to recite six lines of any poem we knew, and I recited her the whole of

Joaquin Miller's "Columbus," "without"—Miss Temby cried in consternation and pleasure—"without a *single* mistake!" and the second time when I wrote her a theme about getting half-buried in a cave-in in the coyote-dug foothills above the Whitemud River. I really believe she was the first person who ever indicated that I might have a literary career.

But I never forgave her, even when she praised me, for when it most mattered, she had laughed, and invited the class to laugh; and laughter is the bitterest of all disparagements, unarguable, irresistible, not to be countered or palliated.

When the three-twenty bell finally rang, light-years after I had come so happily out of the principal's office, I waited until the room had cleared, and then went outside. But I hadn't waited long enough. There was the kid in the sweater, the other kid with the lunch. I started to walk past them, they started to encircle me to have some fun. But right out of the blue, a rough, hoarse, just-changed voice said, "Lay off! Let him alone." I turned around, and there was the big kid who sat behind me, the one as big as a man and in need of a shave. He held out his hand, and after a minute the kid with the sweater pulled it off and handed it over. The one with the lunch passed it like a football. Jeering, but not very sure of themselves, they let us walk away together.

"Where you live?" this man-sized kid said to me.

"Fourth Avenue North."

"You're on my way. Come on."

He walked me home, saying next to nothing. He lived in Little Chicago, across the river; his father worked at the smelter. I realize now, though I didn't then, that his natural way home was a long streetcar ride, and that by walking with me, he was giving himself a three-mile hike. Humble, grateful, proud to be seen with him, I went along with him to our street and our house, and there at the beginning of our sidewalk told him so long, see you tomorrow. I did not thank him, though I was fully aware of what he had done for me. I had a feeling thanks would make him uncomfortable. And I did not tell my mother about him. I didn't tell her much about the day, though she was curious, and kept inquiring. I went into the dining room and sat at the table and did my homework, hating the thought of tomorrow but determined that, since I had to go back to that place, I was going to be prepared for anything Miss Temby might ask.

That big boy, six feet tall and out-weighing me by at least a hundred pounds, is the thing I most want to retain out of that year's school. Without knowing much of anything, I sensed that, coming from Little Chicago, he was second-class, like me. Maybe he too understood that we had inferiority in common, maybe he just accepted, out of pure good nature and decency, the role of protecting a runt. Even on days when he walked home with me, he rarely said much, but he listened while I told him about my gopher-killing prize, and about my trapping, and about the homestead, and about the Whitemud River. I was grateful for his friendship; he was my first friend in Great Falls.

Like everything else that I encountered in that Great Falls year, he taught me a lesson. He taught me that friendships, whether they should do so or not, change with circumstances, and that they involve obligations that we don't always live up to.

By the time I began to feel confident in the eighth-grade room, and got my hand to flapping to beat others in answering Miss Temby's questions, it had begun to dawn on me that my friend, whose name was Joe Something, something Polish or Bohemian—Sedlacek? Sokolski?—was not only the biggest boy in the class but the slowest. He had been kept back about as much as I had been pushed ahead.

Sometimes I helped him with his homework, though generally he just shrugged, indicating either that he didn't intend to do it, or couldn't do it even with help. When anyone bothered me, I looked for him; and I was not above using his name as a threat. But I confess that before very long I felt superior to him. I knew a mixture of shame and impatience when he was paralyzed by one of Miss Temby's questions. Sometimes I whispered answers to him, or passed him the answer on a note, and once I got caught. "Irre*spon*sible, Wallace!" Sometimes, even with the answer in his hand or still echoing in his ear, he still managed to fumble it. Sometimes the class laughed at his dumbness. Sometimes I did, too, incredulous that he could not see what was so plain, or remember what had just been said to him.

Nevertheless, my friend, my protector, my Fidus Achates. Our symbiosis lasted until about Thanksgiving, when he simply stopped coming to school. Perhaps he was dragged off by his migrant family, perhaps he was simply hopeless of ever making it. From where I now sit, I know that there were plenty of boys like him, and plenty of families like his, in the mines and smelters of Montana at the beginning of the twenties. They had linguistic problems, or they had had only the most irregular schooling, or they had to drop out to work. But of all the lessons that I learned, one on top of another, in my first year in civilization, the one Joe taught me—the lesson of kindness and human decency, unmotivated by anything but good nature and goodwill—is the one I most value.

It shames me now that I can't remember that decent, humble, suffering fellow's name.

GLORY HOLES

Patrick Dawson

On my paper route there were many mansions. They were built by lucky mining men and merchant princes during Helena's good days. It was among these personal monuments that I wandered early one snowy fall morning lugging canvas bags of heavy Sunday newspapers from out of state for my far-flung customers. At that moment, I was probably ignoring the faded Victorian splendor in favor of the Detroit architecture of fins, tail-lights, and chrome grilles on autos nudged against old granite hitching posts.

In a flash, my quiet meandering was interrupted by a big blast from across Last Chance Gulch. It slugged the air like a fist and shook the crumbling brick sidewalks. A cloud of dirty white smoke lazily rolled over the tops of the timber. What happened was, some students from the School of Mines at Butte dynamited their rival Carroll College's white-washed-rock letter C off the face of the mountainside. The Orediggers football team had lost the game the day before, but, dynamite being less abstract than football, the engineers and geologists scored an extra point on the philosophers and theologians.

A few years later, the Orediggers finally ended their long losing football streak during the fall of my freshman year at the Butte college. It was cause for celebration, which included, naturally, booze and explosives. With spring came those Sunday afternoons when some of us would convoy over to the desolate rocky hills west of the school for beer and dynamite parties. We blew stuff up and theorized about carrying on the tradition of intercollegiate vandalism. Maybe the big M hanging above the campus at Missoula . . .

The dynamite sticks, fuse, and caps were brought up in student lunch boxes from weekend shifts in the underground mines. The beer came from the taverns of Butte, where it didn't matter if miners happened to be minors. In other towns, setting off explosives and underage drinking might be illegal, but this was Butte, a city built on top of holes, stopes, raises, shafts, and tunnels.

Hardrock mining was risky business. Historically speaking, it therefore followed that it also should be an adventure that might pay off big. After all, according to our license plates back then, Montana was still the Treasure State. There was treasure to behold, at times, a mile down in the Mountain Con, when you are eighteen and surrounded by veins of shimmering peacock copper and pink manganese. Your neck, face and wrists basted in layers of sweat, rock dust, and black drill exhaust. Your senses fine-tuned by the adrenaline-releasing murmurs of shifting slabs and the sickly sweet smell of fir timbers fermenting in the moist heat. But dynamite headaches, dirty lungs, and mangled pardners paid no bonus and promised no bonanza. The treasure belonged to The Company.

The older Butte miners would not allow their young sons to work underground. "Get outa dis whorehouse while ya still can, kid," they advised. Only the transplanted West Virginians in their fluted black lamp hats thought nothing of taking down all the able-bodied menfolk in the clan. This is what they had fled the coal mines for. This, I decided, was not adventure in the tradition of the 1864 Last Chance Gulch prospectors. This was heavy industry.

It seemed a simpler and more exciting proposition back when those lusty prospectors roamed the mountains and creekbeds presuming to strike it rich and free themselves from a future of servitude. There was a promise then, if not of easy riches, then at least of freedom and adventure in a big, unspoiled country hardly scratched by their glory holes. Back then, there were still possibilities.

My own paternal grandfather, born 110 years before me, had wandered the West when it was barely white, and had struck it pretty good as one of the first prospectors into the Black Hills of South Dakota. Just because the Sioux and Cheyenne had exclusive use of the area by treaty with the United States didn't slow down the tide of goldseekers. There was plenty of room for everyone, somewhere.

Grandpa Jack, we gather from all the stories, was seldom bored in those days. One of his friends during his sojourn in Deadwood and Lead was a good pistol shot six months older than he named Bill Hickok. He was the law and nobody jumped Jack's claim. Finally, Grandpa Jack and his partners sold out to the Comstock interests, and Grandpa, the story goes, had one last fling out in San Francisco and then headed for Montana to find his brother. He was about fifty when he quit his wandering to settle down on the Boulder River in Jefferson County, marry a young daughter of the Confederacy and father the first of their thirteen children.

Still, the old man, now a rancher of sorts, couldn't get gold fever out of his blood. He took the older boys poking around the mountains above the valley and one day found an exquisite chunk of gold ore just lying on the ground. Way up a narrow canyon, he staked a claim, built a cabin six logs high, and, working by candlelight, punched a drift back into some rocky slope. I imagine him hitching up a rig every summer and leaving behind the babies and women and heat and mosquitoes and hayfields of the valley. He never did find the motherlode, but it was the seeking that kept him going right up until he died in 1921 at the age of eighty-four.

Growing up around Helena, I had always liked the story of Tommy Cruse, the poor Irish prospector whose requests for a grubstake were rejected by the local Masonic bankers. He struck it anyway, the silver lode that became the great Drumlummon Mine of Marysville. Cruse built a grand house in Helena, of course, and financed much of the building of St. Helena Cathedral. To rub it in a little further, he also started his own bank. To this day, Tommy Cruse has the biggest tombstone in the valley.

It was that legacy of sumptuous physical evidence that helped overstate the American Dream in Montana. The trouble was, it had evaporated by the time my father was born. What remained were the tailings of the frontier boom—the mansions, ghost towns, sagging mill buildings, dredged-out creek bottoms, and the abandoned glory holes. Most of the wealth was long gone, borne away in bullion to more civilized points by the Copper Kings. We inherited their legitimized offspring—one company that ran the mines, smelters, sawmills, courts, and newspapers. Thousands of Montanans became accustomed to having a higher authority control their daily lives. The adventure was over.

Still, the sons of the Argonauts couldn't quite shake the spell. I grew up intrigued by Bill, an old gyppo miner down the road who was always putting together some deal. One corner of his horse pasture was piled with rusting ore cars and rails, spools of wire rope, hoist engines, slusher buckets, and dump trucks missing all glass. It was he who explained to me the origin of the deep shaft up the hill behind our house. It was such a mysterious, spooky hole that I was sure it had once yielded great wealth. But, like many projects around Helena, it was purely political. During the election of 1894, he told me, when Montana voters were to choose between Helena and Anaconda for the state capital, W. A. Clark brought hundreds of men to Helena and put them to work on this glory hole that showed only traces of low-grade copper. Clark made sure they were all registered to vote. Once the votes were counted and Helena won, the hole was abandoned. The surrounding ground became a fantasyland for child miners who dug out green-stained rocks and imagined themselves to be Copper Kings.

A kid had to get that bug somewhere. Grown men like Bill still believed those hills had it in them to make a determined man rich. And I was about five when my father shifted the old truck into compound low and drove us straight up the side of a mountain to check on his claim. There was only wind, clouds, a shallow prospect hole, and a scraggly pine tree on which he had nailed up a flat Sir Walter Raleigh tobacco can stuffed with his location notice. He named the claim the "Mary-Pat," after my sister and me. Like jazz compositions, boats, and bucking horses, mining claims must be named something.

Then there were the wild jeep rides on lower ground, kicked off by the postwar uranium boom. Dad and I hiked through the red rocks and junipers, poking the borrowed geiger counter into holes, just waiting for the loud rush of static that signaled weapons-grade ore. That one never hit. Nor did our unscientific expedition of uncles and cousins ever find the alleged lost silver mine in the high country. It contained ore of such high grade that the old timer who mined it, they say, carried the chunks out on his back, shipped it hundreds of miles by wagon, and still made a profit. We had a great time, though, talking up big plans for our mine when we found it. We even tossed some names around.

No, we never struck it, but it was something to do in that country when it wasn't hunting season. Even while tracking elk up there in snow we whispered about the lost silver mine. I don't know if the grownups were ever really serious about all that prospecting and chasing of legends. I suspect it was in their blood, passed on by Grandpa Jack, and it was a quest that for a while transcended the corporate taming of their Montana. I do know that as soon as my dad was able to draw Social Security, he was out in the hills working his placer claims about every day. Kept him busy, he said. Fresh air, exercise. Just enough flakes and colors to keep it interesting. Some men his age golfed. He shoveled dirt off bedrock and panned it for gold.

It seems that a lot of us native Montanans can't quite shake the illusion that the land still holds promise. We are seduced by our patches of wilderness, the open prairies, the thundering summer waters from the high snowpack, and most of all by our own brief history. There are moments and places when we feel we know what it was like here before barbed wire and steel rail and asphalt lacerated the valleys and plains. It jolts our senses just often enough to keep us too dumb to leave the state for real opportunity. Our imagined prospects are always better, anyway, and we keep waiting, looking, dreaming. Maybe we should know better. Like when Grandpa Jack and his brother Tom first rode into the mouth of the Boulder Valley. The two Irishmen stopped at some running spring water. Tom dismounted, took the tin cup off his saddle, and dipped himself a drink. He promptly spat it out and observed to Grandpa, "We must be gettin' close to hell, Jack—the water's hot!" But they rode on, and settled about twenty miles down the river from the present site of Boulder Hot Springs.

My mother's family came out later, when there wasn't so much left of the promise. This time, the excitement came not from rumors of gold and silver rock, but from the pitches of railroad boosters and land agents. It was to be the last glimpse of Thomas Jefferson's vision of a nation of farmers.

My grandmother once told me that she saw railroad posters back in Iowa depicting a farmer plowing up silver dollars from the prairie soil of Montana. The railroad had an interest in populating the empty land along its lines west, and it was looking to take some suckers for a ride to Paradise.

So they came, with their teams of horses and their piano loaded in a boxcar. My grandmother was twenty-one and single when she got off the train at Miles City in August of 1911 and headed forty miles north to stake out her 320 acres and put up her shack. Then she and her sister returned to Sioux City for the winter and came back out in May. A week later, their homesteads were buried by ten-foot snowdrifts from a three-day storm. At that moment, she recalled later, she would have headed back to Iowa, if only she'd had the price of a train ticket.

One luxury was the coal they hauled in a wagon from an outcropping. She said it beat wandering around the prairie gathering up old buffalo chips. There is a photograph of my grandmother taken in November of 1911, in long dress and heavy wool coat, bending over a chunk of coal outside the door of her tarpapered shack, her mittened hands wrapped around a pickhandle. The caption says, "Wanted: A Man."

She stuck with it, she and her aging parents and older brother and sister. Their homestead claims adjoined, and they built their prove-up houses within shouting distance on the corners. The women made flowers and raspberry bushes grow out there. In good years, they raised dryland hay and grain. One summer, the grasshoppers were so thick that they couldn't hang out their laundry.

Their old-time Methodist backbone kept them on that land. Nobody or nothing was going to take it away from them or drive them out. Not blizzards, grasshoppers, drought, or range hogs. They raised their crops and livestock and went to town in a horse-drawn wagon once a year. It was a challenging place for greenhorns to attempt agriculture.

In 1914, Grandma found an older cowboy still running free out there. Her father, a retired preacher, performed their marriage under the prairie sky on the Rosebud-Custer county line. The couple's dream of turning their homesteads into a cattle and sheep ranch was short-lived. By 1919, Grandpa Sam was so stove-up with rheumatoid arthritis that they moved into town and stayed there.

Grandma's older brother and sister hung on out there for forty years, outlasting most of their original neighbors, then sold out and moved their weary bones to the warmer desert of Arizona. After homestead life in the Big Open, that was living. They retained the homestead's mineral rights. Someday, we'll drill oil wells out there.

The sight of slow brown creeks and yellow gumbo buttes in that country tended to nauseate me when I was a kid. The summer nights were hot and there wasn't even the speck of a cool mountain range on the horizon. It was a different Montana than home. The rocks seemed all the same—there were few trees and I had never been around sheep before. But one rainy teenage summer when the prairie bloomed I came to appreciate a beauty without granite cliffs and waterfalls. At night, I was plagued with aural hallucinations from riding among sheep all day, and it took my intestines a week to get used to the alkaline water. Came summer's end, I rode back to Helena on the train with a better sense of the land and its people. But I still couldn't figure out why my ancestors settled there in the first place.

Years later, I traveled that part of the state often and saw the ranches change from cattle and sheep grazing to grain farming. By the early 1980s, a new kind of land boom was on—sodbusting. Grassy rangeland was plowed up by the township, mostly for tax shelters for big absentee investors. The federal government's farm program subsidized the costs of

PATRICK DAWSON

production, then later paid the sodbusters not to plant again. A drought
dragged on for five or six years and grain prices went to hell. Eastern
Montana farmers and ranchers filed bankruptcy papers and moved to
town. Shades of the Dirty Thirties. Those bare, dusty fields bore a disturbing resemblance to the dried-up gold-mill tailings ponds farther west.

Down at Rosebud Creek and along the Tongue River, King Coal
brought the boomers. Some ranchers liberated themselves from the bitter
cycle of drought and winter feeding by selling their land to the strip-
miners. Some said "Never!" and meant it. Coal-fired power plants poked
strobelight-blinking smoke stacks into the sky and for a moment created
thousands of blue-collar big shots.

And you should have seen the parade of shysters that Cadillacked
their way across the Crow and Northern Cheyenne reservations promising per-capita riches. Just vote for our deal, they told the gatherings of
poker-faced tribal members, and rescue yourselves from prairie ghetto
poverty.

Tribal officials were wined and dined in Washington, Houston, and
Denver. The Billings airport bustled with beaded and braided jet-setters
toting new brief cases. An "Indian OPEC" was promised by pin-striped
opportunists scurrying to tie up tribal resources all over the West.

That rush of hustling was hard on the Cheyenne. Long-time friendships were strained by debates over whether to mine coal and drill for oil
on the reservation. By the white man's standards, they didn't have
much, but they still had their land.

During the 1982 Sun Dance, the sacred ceremony of sacrifice and re-
newal, I stood with my friend Bearcomesout and his little son as the
painted dancers emerged from the Lodge on the last day for the rising of
the sun. There is no easy explanation for the lump in my throat and the
welling up of emotion I felt as the sun slowly whirled above the pine
ridge and the Cheyennes prayed. Was it a sadness for the sunset of their
old ways in the face of progress? Was I moved because the white man
had somewhere lost connection with his own elements?

Later that morning, we drove from Lame Deer to Colstrip to find a store open where we could buy a can of coffee. The road passed between the monster dragline shovels humming in the coal pits. It seemed there was some mechanized alien cancer poised on the edge of Cheyenne country, chewing its way toward sacred ground.

Grandpa Jack went to the Black Hills to find his gold. In the process, the Cheyenne were pushed out of their special place. Every rush for gold, land, water, and coal ends with somebody displaced and disoriented and the planet altered. For a while, times are good and things are rolling. Then it fizzles for almost everyone. It makes it harder for many of us to go on chasing the dream when every so often our destiny is revised by uninvited forces.

From the way they practice their medicine and revere their children it is evident that many of the besieged Cheyenne people are more adept than we at handling such revision. Through it all, they can still look to tomorrow, because they are here today.

As I write this, my daughter is a few weeks old. I noticed right away that the baby was intent on living. You could see it in her moving eyes and in the way she kicked. She is the fifth generation of her line to come into this country called Montana. It would be nice if she lives to see the day when the land starts to heal and its people smile with recognition when the sun comes up. I guess we can't stop dreaming, can we?

4 CULTURAL MATTERS

WAHKPA CHU'GN

Mary Clearman Blew

In Havre the wind is constant. It roars out of the west over the Milk River bluffs, sandblasting every exposed surface—walls, streets, faces—with stinging particles of frozen grit and snow in winter and dust in summer.

The last three years I lived in Havre were drought years, and from my office in Cowan Hall I could watch the sky to the west and see the dust storms rolling ahead of the wind, great banks of topsoil on the move. During the worst of the storms, fine layers of dust would seep in around the closed windows and rise on sill, desk, papers, everywhere, unstoppable, oppressive. It was worse than the dry years of the thirties, some of the older ones were saying, and I felt their apprehensiveness, their compulsion to keep an eye on the west horizon. Havre was changing. The community was sinking into recession, and Northern Montana College, where I had taught so long, had been cut back severely. There had been layoffs, and friends were leaving. I knew by then that I would be leaving, and it was easy to imagine the very landscape filtering in to bury all traces of us.

The dust storms were grim enough in themselves without arming them with an imagined symbolic significance. The streets sometimes were so dark with dust that traffic moved with headlights, and no one walking could have cracked open an eye to see from one curb to the other. In Havre, however, no one walks. Everyone drives, even on errands of a few blocks. Havre is a town of three-quarter-ton, four-wheel-drive trucks, Blazers, Wagoneers, and Lincoln Continentals, last emblems of the glory days of oil and gas development along the highline and five-dollar-a-bushel wheat. One person per vehicle, cruising along in an up-holstered steel chamber, solitary and sealed against the wind and the extremes of temperature that can range from a minus 50° in the winter to plus 110° in the summer. Those customized windows that reflect only some scenic panorama to the onlooker, but which (I suppose) the concealed driver can see out of, are popular.

Ironically, during the last summer I lived in Havre I went on a walking tour. I had known for years that there was a prehistoric buffalo jump site on the Milk River, had heard it was worth seeing, a remarkable site of its kind, unique even, but generally ignored like so much else on the highline that is unique. For years I had intended to visit the site, and finally, under the spur of a visiting aunt and the knowledge that my time in Havre was running out, I phoned for the times of the guided tours, loaded my aunt and my nine-year-old neighbor, Jennifer Larson, into my car, and drove west of town to the museum.

North of Highway 2, just out of Havre on the bluff over the river, lies a Holiday Village, one of the new expansion developments of the seventies. The Village's sprawl is shrunken by the endless sky, like everything else on the highline that rears its silhouette above the horizon, and already it looks shabby from its load of stale merchandise and from getting the brunt of the wind that rolls tumbleweeds and dust across its acres of pavement. Even its colors have bleached down to the pale, permanently windbent grasses in the borrow pits and the ochres of gravel. And across from the Village, south of the highway, lie the equally windswept and faded Hill County fairgrounds, a public park where tourists can camp overnight inside a small shelterbelt of Russian olives and caraganas on irrigated green grass, and the Clack Museum.

On the highline, the summer evenings seem to go on forever, and at seven this evening, when I park outside the museum with my aunt and Jennifer, the sun still is high and brilliant, and the air is heavy. The wind has subsided, as it sometimes does in the late day, but it rags at the weeds and whines off the white siding on the museum. Bicyclists and campers with trailers are beginning to turn into the park and stake their claims, setting up their tiny transitory community of strangers for the night. And outside the front door of the museum, obviously waiting for something to happen, stand a small group of people.

We get out of the car and wait with them. There is a young, tanned couple, and two middle-aged couples with cameras, and a young man with a vacation beard. Clearly, Jennifer and I are the only locals; even my Montana-born aunt has lived out of state for years.

A few minutes pass. Jennifer, indifferent to adult embarrassments, wanders over to a rack and begins a comprehensive selection from its free pamphlets and brochures. My aunt, the only one present to reveal any delight in anticipation, waits with her hands clasped behind her back and her eyes sparkling. Then the screen door opens and bangs shut, and down the steps bounds Elinor Clack.

Elinor counts us. She is about four feet ten, dressed in blue jeans and a jacket, with short gray curls and bright blue eyes. Although she and I have been acquainted for years, she gives me no special sign of recognition; she is being professional, and we all feel better for it. We straighten, gather around. Despite her shortness and her lateness, Elinor is a stiffening breeze. Nothing under her charge could possibly be slipshod or half-hearted or embarrassing.

"Okay," she says. "Back in your cars. We meet down by the entrance gate to the jump site. Anybody want to ride with me?"

The bearded young man accepts her offer. He is a bicyclist, traveling by himself. Elinor gives directions to the rest of us: back east on Highway 2 as far as the city water plant, turn north and then west again on a dirt road we will find deliberately unmaintained, follow it for a quarter of a mile until it ends at the jump site, just under the bluff from the shopping mall.

We climb back in my car and follow Elinor's small convoy down the hill toward Havre, past the water plant, and west along the Burlington

Northern tracks and the river. Jennifer and my aunt lean forward in their seats. They can hardly wait, they are eager for whatever is to be seen, but I keep my eyes on the road, which indeed is badly rutted from the last rainstorm, months and months ago. Below us coils the river, shrunken back from its banks and sandbars by irrigation pumps and drought, and above us looms the bluff.

We are last in line, and by the time I have pulled over on the grassy knoll and parked, others are out of their cars and hiking up the path to the chain-link fence. Elinor is unlocking a massive padlock.

"Vandals," she explains briefly. "We have a terrible problem with vandalism. It's why I don't keep that road maintained."

Here under the bluff the wind is thwarted, and the air is still and warm. Sounds are muted. There might not be a highway above us, or a shopping mall, only sky and overgrown cutbank. Mica sparkles, the river sparkles. For a breath, in the small sounds of shoes crunching on shale and the snapping of grasshoppers, in the smell of river mud and ripe grass and sagebrush, I am back in the Montana of my childhood, with real earth under my feet and real sky over my head. If anything in our experience has permanence, it is the prairie, with its pale turn of seasons, the quiet cycle of the grasses, the shadows of the sky; and for a stabbing moment I wonder how I can leave it. I look to see if anyone else has felt its summons, but they are following Elinor up the ruts that lead to the first house. Even the polite young couple is listening to her commentary.

The Wahkpa Chu'gn site derives its name from the traditional Assiniboine name for the Milk River: the "middle" river, between the Missouri and the Bow. The site is fenced in chain link and stretches over a few hundred yards between the bluff and the river. All that can be seen, except for a glimpse of the roof of the shopping mall and the tops of its green dumpsters at the crest of the bluff, is grass and fencing and the houses. Literally, houses, painted white, with eaves and windows, about twelve feet wide by sixteen long. They remind me of the house on my grandmother's homestead.

Anywhere else—just across the border at Fort Walsh in Alberta, Can-

150

ada, for example, or along the tourist trails in western Montana—this site would have been developed. Structures and facilities would have been designed. There would have been a plan and organization to bring it under control, and strategies to market it skillfully. Nothing would have been permitted to remain an embarrassment for young couples from the east on their way to the West Coast.

But not here, not on the indifferent highline. The small structures that shelter the exhibits were built by Elinor Clack's own hands, and by the hands of members of the Milk River Archaeological Society, which describes itself as "a serious group of amateur archaeologists." These serious people paid for most of the materials themselves and built what they knew how to build: houses.

In fact, the site today looks much as it would have looked two thousand years ago when prehistoric Indian hunters first drove bison over the bluff to be killed and butchered. Elinor says that, over the two-thousand-year span, erosion has blunted the angle of the bluff and raised the floor of the coulee as much as twenty feet with soil buildup over the buffalo bones. Certainly in comparison with museum panoramas I have seen that depict sheer hundred-foot cliffs with tiny dark plasticine figures suspended head over tail in midair, this drop seems undramatic. Inadequate, even. Would it really kill a buffalo to drive him across the Holiday Village parking lot and run him over this bluff? I could easily ride up it, or down, on horseback, and I see doubts on other faces. But allow for erosion, says Elinor, and then consider the evidence of a corral structure in the upper Exhibit A area. The prehistoric hunters would have counted on the corral at the base of the bluff to hold stunned or injured buffaloes until they could kill them with arrows. Nothing dramatic about it, just bloody day-to-day living.

Elinor unlocks the door of the lower house and we all file into a dim stifling room of raw joists and stand around the oblong pit, like a cellar hole, in its center. The pit smells musty and overused, like a cellar, and its floor is littered with fragments of bone that drain away talk. As my eyes adjust to the dusty light from the window in the eaves, I see that bone fragments protrude from the walls of the pit; that, in fact, we have been walking all along on a mound of bones.

"The pit exposes cultural layers from three archaeological phases," explains Elinor. "The deepest bone layers represent the Besant phase. Radiocarbon analysis establishes the earliest Besant use of Wahkpa Chu'gn at 50 B.C. Evidence from other bison kill sites indicates it was at that time—two thousand years ago—that prehistoric hunters of the northern plains developed the bonds and skills needed for communal hunting."

Everyone stands in silence around the charnel. Jennifer, a glutton for all knowledge, is taking slow notes. Then we all file out behind Elinor and follow her up the grassy slope to the next exhibit.

The next house is built into the side of the bluff. Under its eaves the earth has been pared away to expose the faint layers of dun and gray and ochre that mark the succession of cultures buried under our feet. Elinor points out a faint black ring.

"Fire," she explains. "The lower exhibits were kill sites, but this was a campsite. Up here, under the eaves, we've excavated a fire hearth. Would anyone like to climb up and take a look?"

A pause. The steps look precarious, the location of the hearth dusty and obscure under the eaves. Some of the women are drawing back. One wipes her perspiring face with a tissue.

"Oh, yes, I would!"

My aunt dodges out of her place in line and climbs up cautiously. We can see her wrinkled face under her white mop of hair as she peers into the excavation. She hangs up there for the space of several breaths, intent as though she can smell the smoke of the cooking fires, before she lets go and climbs down again. Jennifer is right behind her to take the next turn.

"How old did you say that hearth was?"

"About a thousand years old."

Now, of course, we all climb up to take a look. When it is my turn, I stand on the wobbling step and look into a scraped-out hollow of earth in the stifling heat under the eaves. Plainly it has been blackened by fire, as though yesterday, except for the absence of dead embers. Gradually I understand my aunt's intensity; it is as though, perhaps in one more breath, or in another breath after that, I will catch a whiff of charred wood and cooked meat and even of the steadily working hands that feed the fire and drop the heated stones into the skin water pot. It eludes me; all I really can smell is packed and dessicated earth, but the sense remains that the smoke is there, pungent, drifting, just out of reach. Elinor, watching me from the sunlit doorway, smiles.

"Whew!" says one of the men, mopping his face once we are outside again.

"Imagine what it must have been like a thousand years ago," says Elinor. "Alone about this time in the evening, with the sun going down and the smoke rising from the fires—"

"And the flies! And can you imagine the smell?" he interrupts. "It would have been like a slaughter yard. A slaughter yard is what it was."

"Yes. It was a slaughter yard and a meat-processing plant. They came here to kill buffalo and make pemmican. Evidence from buffalo fetal bones shows constant occupancy, particularly in winter."

It would have been familiar. Home. Coming back year after year, bringing the children and the old people to kindle fires here and prepare for the buffalo drives, a cycle broken only by death. A sense of what it would have been to live in such permanence is as elusive as the vanished smoke.

"Across the river," says Elinor, "may have been their burial places. The river was wider then, and shallower—you can see the marks of the prehistoric channel—and they could have waded across it."

We all look across the mile of river bottom, dotted with cottonwoods and irrigated alfalfa. The line of bluffs to the north are bare and bleached, unaltered since the retreat of the glaciers, and no more remote than those Besant or Avonlea women butchering or tending their fires while their children hunted for berries along the coulee. Their two thousand years, after all, reduces Havre's time here to a shrug.

"How did this site ever come to light again?" asks the bearded young man.

"A schoolboy named John Brumley found it in 1961. He had heard a local story about how the railroaders had dug through tons of bones when they were building the railbed, and so he rode out here on his bicycle and looked. Later he watched the archaeologists and worked beside them and became expert himself."

There remain the actual kill sites to be viewed. Elinor leads us farther up the coulee to the exhibit houses at the base of the drop. By now we are prepared for the close air and stifling heat, the dim light over the excavation pit, the encrustation of bones in the earth walls. But the kill sites elicit several drawn breaths. Even knowing what to expect, who could have dreamed of so many bones? Bones, tons of bones, fragments of bones in endless chaotic pattern, embroidering the layers of sifted dust and earth washed down from the coulee walls, bones, bones deeper than we are tall.

Elinor explains how the hunters drove the buffaloes from the high plains around the buttes, hazing them over a period of several days into drive lanes of stones and piled-up brush that gradually narrowed as they neared the bluff. Then, at the chosen moment, an uproar from the hunters; yelling, waving buffalo ropes, noise, stampeding the enormous animals into a panicky gallop over the brink.

She shows us the traces of post holes, two or three feet apart, that would have outlined the round corral at the base of the drop. Each post hole would have contained two upright posts, wedged in place by ceremonial buffalo skulls. One of these skulls remains in the pit, intact, somehow surviving the years of neglect after the coming of horses to the plains Indians revolutionized their hunting and made the buffalo jumps obsolete, then the years of erosion, the damage of the railroad, and finally the vandals.

"Vandals," says Elinor, locking each heavy door carefully behind us. "I don't know how many windows and doors I've had to replace."

"Looking for souvenirs?" guesses one of the men.

"Well—yes. More than that, they seem bent on destruction. A few years ago, I found this door kicked in. The panel broken. That evening I came back with a piece of plywood and a hammer to repair it, and some-one shot at me."

In silence we walk back down the slope to the parked cars. The sun is low now, and briefly the grasses are golden. The wind has relented, and the river holds what is left of its channel and reflects sky and clouds and the tops of the cottonwoods. No one says a word. It is still hot, and the hike has been fatiguing, up and down the steep slope. Then too, the site imposes its own burden. Something here is as oppressive in its own way as the successive layers of earth and bone. After all these years, some spirit still is powerful enough here to warrant destruction, even to the point of firing shots at its guardian, Elinor.

On the drive back to the museum, Jennifer reads through her store of pamphlets. Being Jennifer, by now she probably can tell a Besant-phase arrowhead from an Avonlea, or one from the Old Women's phase. Her lips move slightly as she reads; her face is beaded with perspiration and new freckles. I wonder what she will retain of Wahkpa Chu'gn. Apparently it altered the whole flow of John Brumley's life.

Next to the Clack Museum stands a restored homestead house. A small frame house, painted brown, not unlike the exhibit houses under the bluff and certainly no bigger. None of the relics it contains can be dated much earlier than 1910, when most of the highline was homesteaded. The highline was one of the last of the northern plains regions where remnant Indian populations were pushed off into starvation and death by disease to make way for white settlement. It is a time within living memory, Indian and white.

But apparently these relics are worth stealing or smashing, because the door is locked. The young couple shade the glare of the late sun with their hands to peer in at a window.

"What is that tub with the handle for?" the woman is asking.

"I don't know. Maybe a churn?"

My aunt stops short. "Oh, no! That's no churn! It's a washing machine!"

In the face of their surprise she ploughs on. "My mother had one like it. I remember it perfectly well. You carried water from the boiler on the stove to fill it. Then you put the clothes and the soap flakes in, and you pulled back and forth on that handle"—she points out the handle on the side of the tub, the one that suggested a churn—"until your clothes were agitated. Then you wrung them out and rinsed them, and wrung them out again and hung them out to dry. You drained the water out of your washing machine through a plug in the bottom."

They are staring at her as though she just stepped out of, say, the early Besant period.

"A lot of backbreaking work," the young man murmurs at last.

Something lives on the highline that cannot examine itself. Outsiders recognize its presence but fail to describe it, hurrying instead over the prairie highways at eighty miles an hour to reach the more conventional shadows of the mountains.

Judging from the closed and sullen faces in the old photographs in the museum, the hysterical invective rising from the pages of the earliest newspapers, it has existed here since the first white penetration of the highline. Perhaps it is the quality that perpetrated genocide, or perhaps it is the inevitable outcome of genocide, a kind of mark of Cain.

Whichever it is, it endures, excluding the outside world and yet failing to settle here, failing to call it home. Rather than admit it has a past—and, therefore, guilt—and mortality—it shuts itself away in indifference, or drunkenness, or chauvinism, keeping to itself even among others of its own kind, but ready to lash out on any provocation or hint of a threat. The record of its past is a threat, and Wahkpa Chu'gn is just such a record—of the roots it cannot claim, of the fate it cannot accept.

To live in Havre is to live in a dilemma. Introspection is subversive here, and memory treasonable. And yet it is the brink on which we all live, the blade of the knife pressed against tomorrow. In Havre the wind is constant, but two thousand years are as close as yesterday, and we fail to look back at out peril.

DOLOMITE

Robert Sims Reid

Lately, I've been working on a fictional character who has an interest in geology and palaeontology. It didn't take long for me to reach the point where I needed to know at least some of the things my character claims to know. Field guides did the trick for a while. Sometimes, though, you find that poring over books, like watching basketball on TV, can be a lot of fun, but in the end it helps to go out and work up a good sweat. I'm far from being the kind of expert my fictional character insists I should be, but I was grounded enough on a particular Saturday to put on my hat and get in the truck and head out of town with the dogs and a carpenter's hammer and chisel and get dirty.

Town in this case is Missoula, Montana. I don't want to get too specific about just where I went, but I will say that I drove along a river. You see, one of the rules here in Montana is that we try to avoid telling people precisely where we go when we go out of town. This rule applies to hunting or fishing, cutting firewood or digging for fossils or mineral crystals or prospecting for gold. Normally, we simply avoid answering a question of this kind. When pinned down, we lie. Or, if we feel particularly devious, we tell the truth, knowing that the questioner will assume that we're lying.

I've been referring to Montanans as *we*, but of course that's a lie, too. My daughter can honestly say *We* when talking about Montanans, since she was born in Kalispell. I, on the other hand, have lived here only fourteen years. I was born in Scott County, Illinois, and although I haven't lived there now for half my life, I can still return there and call it home, while people who moved to that tiny place fifty or sixty years ago and worked all their lives there, married there, bore and buried children there, are still seen by others and by themselves as outsiders. *Us and Them* is a notion I understand.

So the dogs and I headed up into the mountains along the river, looking for a limestone or shale outcropping in which to root around for fossils. It was a cloudy spring afternoon, and I ended up driving farther than I'd planned. I passed through areas criss-crossed by motorcycle trails and logging roads. There were houses off in the trees and over the valley below. In places, particularly after I turned up into the mountains away from the river, there were broad clearcuts across the mountainsides. In the distance ahead, I could see a huge power line, the subject of an equally huge public debate in the recent past. By any definition, this was not wilderness. But it was hardly metropolitan, or even what we traditionally think of as agricultural. I guess you could say it was just *country*.

As I write this, there is a photograph above my desk of the farm in Scott County where I spent the first twenty years of my life. Now, Scott County hasn't been wilderness within the memory of anybody still alive. But as I look at that photo, taken in 1987, the farm today seems relentlessly cultivated in a way that is very unlike the farm in my memory from, say 1955, or with what I see in another photograph of that same farmstead, taken before World War II.

The house was built by a man named Giles Reeder in the 1880s. It's a two-story frame farmhouse, the kind you see on countless farms in that part of the country. The house sits about two hundred yards north of the road. In very formal style, the driveway originally ran under the canopy of twin rows of maples straight from the road toward the front door, before making a turn at the gate of the ornamental fence around the yard. The driveway has since been moved twice, to approaches from the east side of the house. The huge maples—at least twenty of them—are all gone.

Until I was eight years old, I lived with my parents and sister in a small gray house about a quarter of a mile from the main place. There were a barn and chicken house there. There was also a third house, which we called the Gordon place. The hired hand and his family lived there. Besides the house, the Gordon place included two barns and two sizable sheds. The gray house, the Gordon place, and all the outbuildings are gone now, too, and modern agriculture has made the farm too small to support a hired hand.

My grandparents lived on the main place. Behind that house there was a smokehouse, where the butchering was done and meat hung above a smoldering pit. We kept the cream separator in this shed, too. Behind the smokehouse lay the garden and a huge pear tree. Next came the chicken house and behind that a brooder house. East of the chicken house were a machine shed, where we stored the farm equipment, and an oil shed. Then there was the barn, full of hay, and behind it a sheep shed, and just down the slope farther east a pond. There was a corn crib too, which was sided with walnut slats. (Imagine that—walnut used for lumber. I still can't believe it.) And, of course, there were portable hog sheds scattered like small camps all over the place.

So you take these four hundred and eighty acres and criss-cross them with fences. Drop in the livestock—beef and dairy cattle, horses, hogs, sheep, chickens, maybe some ducks and dogs—then add several families, snap the whole cluttered concoction to life, and you have your basic agricultural utopia.

Well, maybe.

One thing I do know is that building and keeping the kind of farm I recall wasn't some pastoral lark. It involved brute labor of the sort that most people I know today—myself included—would not do. One of my grandmother's sisters married a gentleman who worked for the electric company in nearby Jacksonville. I'm told that in the days before rural electrification, it was Uncle Hubert's sincere opinion that farmers were too stupid to know what to do with electricity if they had it. If you believe that Thomas Jefferson gave life to a sort of agrarian Everyman, then you might also say that my Uncle Hubert wrote his epitaph.

The first stage of my Saturday fossil expedition didn't come to much. After driving for nearly an hour, I finally came across some sedimentary rock that had been exposed by the road cut. I drove a little higher, until reaching the snowline, then turned back and parked at the upper end of the bed. I let the dogs run while I started in to work.

The rock was a soft reddish brown shale or mudstone, which cleaved easily along bedding planes. I started near the truck, at the highest exposed point of the bed. By raking away debris, I could clear off a surface of rock perhaps two feet square, and then peel away the layers with a hammer and chisel as though turning stony pages.

For me at least, it turned out that the pages were blank. For the next hour or so, I worked my way several million years deeper in the bed by moving back down the road. Sometimes the newly exposed surfaces were a mottled brown and green, like an indistinct film of wet leaves. This observation, however, involved color rather than any individual impression. While a true palaeontologist, or a micropalaeontologist might well have been able to make something of those rocks, nothing ancient and dead jumped out at me and said, "Here I am."

By the time I got back to the truck, I was hearing rifle and pistol shots from the canyon below. A little Saturday afternoon recreational gunplay. Nothing uncommon, no cause for alarm. I loaded up the dogs and headed down.

Even in my earliest memory, the smokehouse was unused. I should have taken that as a sign of things to come, but conflicts of evolution versus decay seldom arise—and never with urgency—before middle age.

We traded houses with my grandparents when I was in the third grade. My mother was pregnant again and we were on the verge of outgrowing the small gray house. The ornamental fence was gone by that time, and the towering maples one by one gave way to wind or disease and were not replaced. The sheep shed was torn down after my father, in an act of defiance, sold all the sheep one winter while my grandfather was out of town. The work horses were sold, too, though we kept the last foal, a wild painted mare with soft feet, until she died barren of old age. I guess it made us feel good to watch her race across the pasture ahead of a thunderstorm.

Soon the milk cows went, and later the beef cattle. Portable hog sheds gave way to a confinement operation, in which the hogs were raised on platforms in a tightly enclosed area, which strikes me now as more like running a meat factory than farming. Eventually, the hogs were all sold, too.

Today, the house remains. And the barn, though it's empty now, more suitable for use by a sentimental landscape artist than a farmer. The machine shed stands idle, replaced by a metal building large and ugly enough to accomodate modern machines. The walnut slats have been peeled off the corn crib and replaced by sheet metal. A cylindrical grain bin of corrogated steel has been added. All the rest, the oil shed and chicken house, the brooder house and all the hogsheds are gone. All of the fences are gone, too. Today, no one leaves the house silently at daybreak to move sleepily among sleepy animals.

You must understand that none of this happened exactly on purpose, though it is the current result of hundreds, maybe thousands of decisions, none of which was part of a premeditated plan to destroy our past. When he was a very young man, my grandfather tore down a log house behind the barn before he learned that it was perhaps the first house built in the county. He didn't set out to destroy history. The house was just old and in the way and of no further use. He was just being practical. Everything just happened.

And you must understand that this farm in its present state is *not necessarily* a wrong kind of place, though it is certainly a different kind of place from the one I remember and care about. Actually, today it looks amazingly good. Everything is in fine order . . . no weedy fencerows giving the fields a ragged fringe . . . no sheds to repair . . . no livestock to dig mudholes or stink up the place or escape on Sunday morning and ruin dinner. The first casualty of technology is clutter. I guess you might say our farm looks like it's run by an efficient doctor who only wants to know what your symptoms are and never asks you how you feel.

One night after electricity had come to the country, my grandfather drove by the Gordon place when it was still owned by Gordon. He said that every window in the house was ablaze with light and Scott Gordon himself was sitting in a chair in the front yard, looking back at the house. My grandfather stopped to see what was wrong. He thought the place was on fire.

No, Gordon told him. Everything was fine, just fine. He only wanted to see how she looked with all that electric light.

That was the end, of course, though no one could have predicted it. From the instant it's possible to light every window of a house by pushing buttons, men will become discontent to walk all day behind horses. Women will demand more of their lives than to kill and cook chickens and hoard the loose change from extra eggs and milk sold on Saturdays. Teenagers will never again deny themselves town. We should be stronger people than this, but for the most part I think we are not. I am writing this piece on a computer. I don't feel a hint of shame about not working in longhand.

On my way home, I noticed a chimney rock rising from the coulee to my left. I parked under some spruce trees at a turnout. It was midafternoon and warm there on that bench above the river, though snow squalls smudged several drainages miles away across the valley.

My grandfather always loved the West. For all I know, I may live in Montana as the result of something subliminal I picked up from him, some unknowing nudge on my personality before I was even aware that I had a personality. The view from that bench reminded me of the stories he used to tell about driving through Glacier Park back in the days when automobile travel was still an adventure.

The coulee was too steep and wooded for me to see the bottom, but the chimney rock rose clear about a hundred yards from the bench. The dogs followed me down a path that ran along the top of a saddle of fine sand between the bench and the rock spire, which turned out to be an outcropping of very hard sandstone, and not what I would describe as a true chimney. The bare and weathered sandstone reached perhaps eight or ten feet above a steep, brushy ridge, which fell away on its north side toward the river. The south edge of the spire ended instantly with a sheer drop of at least a hundred feet to the bed of a dry creek. Then the same rock formation continued in another very steep—though not sheer—wall on the other side of the creek bed. The cut between the two faces is not more than thirty feet wide.

At various times during its geologic history, our valley has been under water. As best my novice eye could tell, the saddle between the bench and the sandstone outcropping was the remains of a sandbar deposited by an ancient river as it flowed around the large section of freestanding rock. Now, in modern times, the relic sandbar diverts intermittent streamflow through the cut, rather than allowing the spring runoff a more direct route to the river.

This may or may not be an accurate account of what happened here over the ages. Given my status as a Saturday-afternoon explorer, it will have to do. I said earlier that we lie out here in Montana about where we've been. The standard explanation for this trait is that we don't want someone else to go there behind us and reap our rightful harvest of elk, fish, gold, or other treasure. I think, though, that we're also motivated by a desire not to know that someone else has been there first, by a need for secret places where the clock does not stop, for there is no clock. Granted, a path means that we are not alone. But an anonymous path lends itself well to solitude.

I found my way down to the dry creek bed along a second path, which branched off the sandy saddle. The slope was covered with brush, but the bed itself was clear, and I followed it toward the river. Around me, the slopes narrowed and steepened until they were finally walls. Once inside this cleft, it was very still, and I felt sealed off from the large country around me, as though I had stepped into a small room with a ceiling of sky.

Along the walls of fractured sandstone, there were eroded cavities, where small animals had made dens. As I examined these cavities, I began to find clusters of sharp, clear dolomite crystals. Dolomite rock is found in many places in North America, though well-formed crystals are not. The crystals sometimes form when seawater seeps through rock and collects in small cavities, where it slowly evaporates. Dolomite has both industrial and medical uses. The crystals are brittle, and cleave perfectly in three directions.

I spent the rest of the afternoon with my tools, rapping on the rock, exposing and following fissures that had never seen the light of day, discovering crystals. Sometimes the crystals occur singly, sometimes in clusters. The largest I found measures less than half an inch on a side. Looking into the bright, translucent interior of the crystals, you see cleavage lines that mirror the smooth exterior surfaces, lines along which the crystal may someday fracture into smaller versions of itself.

You always wait for that moment when the sense of an experience makes itself known, as though the world has made a pact with you to explain itself if you just behave and keep faith.

But I don't have any explanation for the immediate value of a single crystal. No more do I have an explanation for the enduring value of the ambiance of failure that surrounds what I always reckoned to be an agricultural ideal in Scott County, Illinois. Sometimes I believe I have an explanation, when all I really have is another set of questions. It's all part of the geography of my imagination.

One day, the Gordon place really did burn up. Years after the last hired hand collected his last check and packed his family and headed down the road, the place was about as useful as that log house my grandfather had torn down. Somewhere, there may still be a Gordon who resents the hell out of the Reid family for the day we set a match to Scott Gordon's house in order to get another acre of corn. For what it's worth, I offer my apologies, though I'm certain we'd do it again.

It was in a field just to the northwest of the Gordon place where my father lost his left hand in October of 1951, when he reached into a corn-picker to free a jammed stalk and couldn't let go quick enough. He had come to be farming in the first place after my grandfather had a heart attack in 1947, and my father left the University of Illinois to take over the farm. Nobody wanted this, but in 1947, the only cure for a heart attack was permanent rest, and obligations of the land came before all others. I don't remember my father with both hands, and, curiously enough, in nearly all of the pre-accident photographs of him, his left hand is shielded from view.

When I look at the 1987 photograph of our farm, it sometimes seems as though the fields are creeping closer around the remaining buildings, as though the place is slowly being cauterized and someday it will be as though nothing ever happened there. I can lift my eyes into the flat, humid haze on the horizon and find all the reasons for moving West. And, in the treeladen photo from before the War, I see all the reasons why it's so damned hard to go back.

Somewhere along the line, my grandfather became a compulsive saver of things. Everything. Scrap lumber. Bailing wire. Feed sacks. Leather harnesses. Broken machines. Hand-split triangular fence posts, the Lincoln model. In the early sixties he went to an auction and came home with a pickup load of horse collars, at least a decade after the last plowhorse climbed the loading chute. A few years after he and my grandmother built a new brick house across the road from the Giles Reeder place, she made him get rid of the last pile of those wooden fence posts because she got tired of looking at them out the front window. So one day we rounded up five gallons of gasoline and had another big fire. Next spring, the grass came in very green, like it always does. The horse collars are still there. But no horses.

STRAIGHT TO THE ACTUAL

David Long

*I doubt that character and conduct are much shaped by
landscape, climate or geography. We manage
to breed saints, brutes, and mudheads in all sorts of
topographies and climates. But what country does to our way
of seeing is another matter. . . . I respond to the forms and
colors I was trained to respond to, I acknowledge what
revives my memory. But only when I have submitted to a
place totally. Any earth I have shoved around with a
bulldozer will be impotent to stir me. The more power I have
and use, the less likely I am to submit to anything natural,
and the less spiritual power natural things will have over me.*

—WALLACE STEGNER,
"Crow Country"

1

Russell Martin, introducing *Writers of the Purple Sage*, an assemblage
of recent writings from the Rocky Mountain West, argues that the
hugeness of the land makes it "an inescapable literary element." These
writers, he says, "meticulously anchor their tales to terrain, defining

their characters, in part, by describing the land that surrounds them." It strikes me that fiction writers always do that. Even if the locale is less-than-spectacular, even if it's essentially man-made. We pretend the specific trouble we're telling has to happen *there*—if it happened some place else, it would be a different trouble. That's how fiction works—it's tidier, *denser*, than the random misadventure played out in the evening paper. To say it another way: in serious fiction, description is never filler.

Still, Martin's right. This habit of mind, this willingness to illuminate character by way of landscape, seems especially fierce among western-ers. Speaking as one story writer: I can't imagine the people I write about without imagining what they see as they head off to work, lost in small thoughts. Magpies in a low slant over wheat stubble, osprey nesting on the crossbars of the powerpoles. Cottonwood, Lombardy poplar, tam-arack turning rusty in the foothills. Clay dust pluming out in the rear view, and up ahead, any way they're aimed, a skyline ragged with mountains. I'm obliged because it's *their* place, and because, frankly, it *is* spectacular. It intrudes all the time. Nor can I do these characters justice if I don't know how this valley came to be settled, how people contrive to make a living here, how they amuse themselves. None of which makes sense without taking into account the basic geography. For all our turnover of citizenry, for all the turf-fighting and bureaucratiza-tion, it's still what it was: a place where wild space and small-town Amer-ica collide.

But I want to talk mainly about *seeing,* and specifically about how the land works on Montana's visual artists. First, there's a distinction to be made—not exactly ironclad, but serviceable—between "western" and contemporary art. For the sake of argument, "western" being the art most tied to an idealized memory of life in the West. It's mainly nar-rative, a reinforcing art. It gives back, often in splendid detail, what we expect to find there. No surprise, then, that Montana's terrain, at its gaudiest, is recycled tirelessly in these works. What's more interesting is how much it figures in contemporary work.

In the past few years, Montana's arts infrastructure, art centers and museums and commercial galleries, have mounted numerous shows devoted, in one way or another, to how our artists see their home place: "Western Places" (Missoula Museum of the Arts); "Resources: Plenty and Plundered" (The Brunswick Gallery); and "Montana Landscape" (The Hockaday Center for the Arts in Kalispell), to name only a few. Add to this sundry other exhibits and one-person shows devoted to the work of Montanans. In even the most avowedly nontraditional of this work you find a persistent visual reference to the land.

This is not, you understand, urban art.

It may strike us that making pictures of the land is an ancient practice, but in fact it isn't. Not until the latter part of the eighteenth century—one product of the revamped thinking that came with the industrial revolution—did artists, in the European tradition, begin to view the land itself as more than a setting for human affairs, as a power and a source of illumination in its own right. In the West, landscape art began with the public need to document the country's vast acquistion of territory—The Great Reconnaissance, it's been called. Karl Bodmer came west in the employ of Prince Maximilian of Prussia. Painter Thomas Moran and photographer William Henry Jackson worked for the U.S. Geological Survey. Walter Shirlaw was a Special Agent for the 1890 Census. Abby Williams Hill painted for the railroad. Many others, including the likes of Remington and Russell, illustrated for magazines—*Harper's Weekly*, *Century*, and, later, *Collier's*. The public appetite was enormous. It's fitting that the work was mainly faithful to its raw subjects—and we can be as grateful for this record of how things looked in that recently lost time, as outsiders must have been then. But it was the private curiosities of these men and women, their *awe*, that made what they did art. You have only to spend a few minutes with one of Albert Bierstadt's panoramas—*A Storm in the Mountains—Mount Rosalie* (1866), for instance—to see how the documentary urge got tangled in a personal vision. Even among the photographers—Haynes, Curtis, Muybridge, Watkins, and the many others—there was more going on than naked reportage.

If there's one element common to the majority of landscapes, it's the division of the visual field into two zones: sky over earth, the dailiness of weather spread across the quietude of geologic time. There are exceptions—work that's willfully flat or obstructed with walls, shots straight down from airplanes, and so on—but most landscapes let us see clear through to the horizon. The other main pleasure of landscapes is that they aren't pictures of people, even when people are present. In this, they're more Far Eastern in their way of seeing. Take Timothy H. O'Sullivan's *Wall in the Grand Canyon, Colorado River* (1871): down at the bottom of the frame, six human specks, of no greater consequence than the pocks of shadow on the canyon wall.

These elements answer our occasional need to stand planted in a spot and see a long ways, and to drop our desperate fixation with things human. But they threaten, too. Whatever the specific mood of a landscape, there's an emptiness at its heart: the solitariness that comes of being a lone set of eyes aimed at so much that isn't you, that with luck will outlast you by a billion-odd years. "To look upon the ordinary landscape," says photographer Lewis Baltz, "is to gaze into the abyss."

And this emptiness lets us regard, apart from notions of utility, the marks of human habitation. Road cuts, disked-over soil, managed water. . . . We're given the chance to forget what we know—to see beauty or coherence in the inadvertent shapes of our tenancy, and by the same token, to recognize with fresh horror the ugliness of structures we've come to take for granted.

2

Try this for openers: the art of a region begins to come
mature when it is no longer what we think it should be.

—WILLIAM KITTREDGE,
"Doors to Our House"

Readers of Kittredge's essays know how fervently he believes artists need to disentangle themselves from prevailing myth. Where myths were, traditionally, thought to be true stories, told to keep cultures together, to help their citizenry act sensibly, myths about the American West were largely manufactured, only ever true in severely limited ways, and so contradictory as to be no help at all. What we want to do now, Kittredge says, is "see straight to the actual." It's not a new problem. Californian Maynard Dixon, renowned painter and illustrator whose early work was modeled on Remington's, ran afoul of his eastern editors finally—"I'm being paid to lie about the West," he complained to a friend. This was 1912. It was a crisis that returned him home, and launched him into a period marked by both his best painting and an endless scramble to make a living. For *Sunset,* a few years later, he elaborated: "My object has always been to get as close to the real thing as possible. . . . The melodramatic Wild West idea is not for me the big possibility. The more lasting qualities are in the quiet and more broadly human aspects of Western life . . . the poetry and pathos of Western people seen amid the grandeur, sternness, and loneliness of their country."

But what *is* the actual in our time? Wilderness or clearcut? Amber waves of grain or Minuteman silos? How can you be naive again, having seen so much? Specifically: how can you work in a traditional form and do what's not expected?

What's immediately impressive about the contemporary work is its unruliness. There's no one aesthetic, no one attitude or style. Traditional realism stands tooth by jowl with modernist explosions of paint and temperament, as well as various postmodernist articulations—strange mixtures of media, installations, conceptual pieces—that defy quick cubbyholing. Artist to artist, the degree of abstraction changes radically. Many of the visual elements you'd expect to represent Montana do appear, time and again: mountain meeting sky, empty two-lane blacktop, cattle and sheep, horses, grizzly. And there's a general absence of what you'd expect not to find—images of dense human habitation, say. But these elements come with spin. They're taken apart and reassembled in ways that undermine expectation. They give not one calculated shock but repeated shivers.

In his elegantly named little book, *Beauty in Photography: Essays in Defense of Traditional Values,* photographer Robert Adams claims that a landscape picture offers three verities: geography, autobiography, and metaphor. If so, Montana's artists are giving us a great deal of work that comes from the place where autobiography and metaphor merge. The reporting back that nineteenth-century artists did has become, more severely, a reporting back from the individual imagination, from what Kittridge calls "private strangeness." In the place of those received and unreliable myths about the West, artists are offering up personal mythologies.

A taste of what I mean here:

In Kathryn Person Kress's pastel, *Coming Home in the Dark: Blue Bay,* the horse is indeed blue, and enormous, standing in powerful serenity, an icon of the work's mysterious title. In Ted Waddell's paintings, thrusts of black acrylic—abstract, haphazard even, if you're too close—become cows in a winter storm when you stand back. Each pose nailed with an efficiency that seems to transcend technique. As Waddell, who ranches in country north of Billings, says, "I don't make any separation between doing this [the art] and taking care of the cows." Dennis Voss's landscape drawings begin with a suggestion of terrain and hour, but are overlaid with a frenzy of markings and symbolic annotations, which seem to argue that the land is anything but empty—that it's awash with movement, littered with emotional reverberations. Growing up on a ranch in Amsterdam, Montana, sculptor Gary Bates became obsessed with the horizon line of the Gallatin Valley. One result of this fascination is a work called *Horizon 7-Ranges,* nearly two tons of steel set in concrete, a dome with the top torched off. You sit inside on an antique barber chair, chin secured, and you revolve: the edge of the metal makes an exact duplication of the skyline. And if the piece were filled with water, Bates says, "it would flow out precisely where the Missouri River does."

In the twenty-five years since Russell Chatham pulled into Livingston with five dollars in his pocket, he's become the best-known of our contemporary painters, certainly the most written-about. His work has a fierce following—from the bartenders and veterinarians, writer and movie-business friends he bartered it to in earlier times, to, more recently, a gang of upscale collectors. Celebrity aside, Chatham has that quality of concentration, of large achievement, we associate with artists whose endeavors will last.

Chatham works mainly in large oils and lithographs, a stunning example of the latter being the *Missouri Headwaters* series, a dozen huge landscapes chronicling a year by month. He works only from memory, never photographs. Nor are there original paintings for these lithographs. He worked them directly onto zinc plates, using liquid asphaltum or litho crayons, each image requiring upward of forty-seven colors, which is to say, forty-seven separate plates, forty-seven days of printing and drying.

What Chatham paints isn't so much the look of a moment as how a landscape has come to feel after one's long-time immersion in it. It's not the work of someone passing through. Chatham's eye seems fully alive in the most subdued of lights—what my father loved to call the gloaming, a moody, transitional time. The pictures are austere without being somber. In a great many, there's an emergence of light, a glow along a hillside or a sheen on a bend of water, that draws the eye and gives the spirit an unspeakable feeling of hope. This is Chatham's particular gift.

Patrick Zentz grew up to ranch life along the Yellowstone, a hundred or so miles east of Chatham's Paradise Valley. He left Montana for college in the sixties, thinking he'd become a doctor, but gravitated toward artwork, returned and took an MFA in sculpture in Missoula, taught for several years, and eventually settled back at Big Spring Ranch, which adjoins the land he was raised on. Where Chatham's art may be thought of as classical, Zentz's is conceptual, ritualistic. Many of the works include performance, and rely on an array of intricate devices, the one constant being their examination of the land around the ranch. "The concept of translation is very critical to me," Zentz has said. "Changing one thing to another in order to gain access perhaps to either a new perspective on information or a new kind of information."

A recent project was called *Day*. On Labor Day weekend of 1985, Zentz and a crew of friends installed three devices Zentz had spent the winter designing and fabricating—*Horizon Instrument, Creek Instrument, Runoff Drum*—each an ingenious solution to part of the task, which was to turn the effects of natural events on the land's surface into music. Once an hour, around the clock, Zentz fired his gun from a single point and the recorders were turned on, capturing five-minute slices of the day's concert, later mixed into one haunting, minimalist recording included in the project's catalog.

3

Is landscape an *inescapable element* for artists in the West, as Martin claims?

Of course not.

We're mobile, we have an incredible access to ideas from all over, we work in an era that tolerates the idiosyncratic. We can do pretty much whatever we choose, whatever works. Still, you could argue that the influence of the land is oppressive, that all this attention to The Landscape of the American West is tiresome as last year's calendar, an insidious barrier to more illuminating stuff. And you could argue, from another angle, that too little of this work reflects either Montana's troubled history or its present-day economic and social conundrums. You could argue, in short, that even the contemporary work is romantic, devoted so single-mindedly to an individual's vision.

But I'd rather ask: is it necessary to escape this influence? And: what would it cost?

In a recent writing ("Irish Journal") Wendell Berry uses the expression "local intelligence." He's speaking of animal husbandry, but it's a phrase that speaks handsomely to other husbandries. Local intelligence. What a disappointment it would be—a betrayal of a sort—if our artists cut themselves off, *altogether*, from Montana's land and its commonplace images. You see the dilemma, though, how it can seem to an artist—to writers and musicians, as well—that the price of a wider reknown is bowing to a critical establishment that pays no homage to life as we know it here. It's a twist on one of the oldest themes in the Montana story: the local and singular devalued by the placeless and corporate.

In aesthetic terms, there's a fear of the cliché, of common sentiment, giving rise to a lust for originality. And this is satisfied in rather shallow ways sometimes. Innovation is appealing—shocking, titillating even— but it doesn't necessarily mean much. The thing to bear in mind about clichés is that they're generally true—it's only the numbing familiarity that's wrong, not the moment of understanding they embody. *Making it new* doesn't, finally, require isolating oneself from traditional sources of nourishment.

As for the political content of this work (I'm not talking about baldfaced propaganda), it's true that overt social comment is only near the top of a few artists' agendas. In fact, much of the landscape work will seem, at face value, as morally neutral as nature itself. Still, there's a view of nature implicit here, one at odds with other attitudes loose in the land. As Lewis Baltz writes:

> One of the most common views our society has of nature
> is among the most rigorously secular and least appealing:
> landscape-as-real-estate. . . . To know that an
> apparently unbroken expanse of land is, in fact, overlaid
> with a network of invisible lines demarking ownership
> and indicating the pattern of future development is to
> perceive it in another way. That these divisions only
> coincidentally pertain to the topography and are the
> arbitrary result of financial speculation illustrates the
> casually rapacious disdain that our culture has for the
> natural world as such.

In this light, landscape art is preservationist, nonpolluting, a blow against the bureaucratic mind. Though it offers a view of things as they are right this moment (literal or not) it's anything but complacent. It starts in the closest knowledge, what Stegner calls "submitting," which is, of course, where our best politics arise as well.

There was a joke my father used to tell. It ended with a man in a shower stall clutching his clothes and explaining: "Well, everybody's gotta be somewhere!" I loved my father's delivery, his sense of the man's aplomb under fire. But the key to the thing was, the man wasn't where he belonged. People who stray are lively fodder for storytellers, always have been. I started off this essay giving thought to some of the characters I've committed to print over the last few years, and it occurs to me now to say there are stories worth telling about people who stay home, too. Belonging isn't the passive business it's cracked up to be. It's one thing to gawk at the mountain skyline with a tourist's ignorant wonderment, quite another to pay attention over the long haul. For those of us who stay, that's the real work: to find, in practicing our art, ways to renew our awe when it goes dead, ways of seeing the actual in the commonplace.

IN SPITE OF DISTANCE

The New Literature of Montana

Ralph Beer

A television advertisement offers, as part of Montana's upcoming Centennial celebration, a deed to one square inch of Montana and the pitch, "Own a piece of the last of what's best in America." The offer, of course, is pure Chamber of Commerce boosterism taking subdivision to its final extreme. But I'm intrigued by the slogan. I want to believe it even if I'm a little unclear about what it means exactly, an ambivalence most of us share about living in this singular place right now. Admit it, it's hard to name just what, in the vast and radical geographic, economic, and ethnic differences of Montana, gets its hooks into us, gives us an identity and source of pride, even helps create a unique and prolific out-pouring of literature all its own. Yet always we go back, when attempting to name this itch, to place or a sense of place that may not always be connected to any certain spot on the map.

Because Montana is so dissimilar from border to border and from county to county, there must be other reasons for our shared sense of identity and literature besides lists of favorite places. And the foremost of these reasons is, I think, an unconscious but still active sense of the fron-tier—a feeling subtle yet suggestive as a half-remembered dream—that is a response to an accumulation of uniquely American mythology, a brief and recent history, powerful visual remnants of that past, and, most of all, a dramatic landscape. We know, even if we never go there, that the great Beartooth Range rises only a few hours to the east, that only a few miles west the rugged beauty of the Rocky Mountain Front meets the plains still frequented by grizzlies. Rising like sets of magical back-drops, Montana's mountains bear physical witness that we live in a largely unsettled, harsh, and fragile land in the foreground of even wilder, less hospitable distances. And while thousands of satellite dishes aim southward above these mountains, the overpowering presence of dis-tance and the ever-present threat of isolation is for many as real today as for frontier farmers Richard Hugo remembered with the lines:

> Even wind must work when land gets old. The rotting
> wagon tongue makes fun of girls who begged to go to
> town. Broken brakerods dangle in the dirt. Alternatives
> were madness or a calloused moon.

But to go back to what, for white Montanans at least, is both beginning to Montana history and Montana literature, we must begin with Lewis and Clark, who wrote what is largely a record of their sense of wonder at this place. Perhaps in no other document of the early West is the power of place so overwhelming. When Lewis and Clark set out in 1804, Amer-ican attitudes were changing; Jefferson's vision of agrarian pastoralism was spreading before the plows of yeoman farmers in the East, and mar-ried to this vision of pastoralism was the enlightened notion that wilderness was not a dark, unknown place of evil as the Calvinists had held, but a garden, filled with life-giving potential for the nurturing of countless generations of husbandmen. Of course Mr. Jefferson had no idea that the West was largely made up of places like the Sand Hills of Nebraska, the Staked Plains of Texas, the Alkali Flats of Wyoming, or the Bitterroot Mountains of Montana and Idaho, and this oversight brought, just as surely as the Homestead Act and railroads, generations of grief to thousands of sodbusters who shared his dream.

As Lewis and Clark moved upriver, their early journal entries reflect both Jefferson's idea of wilderness as Edenic and their own simple joy to be moving through such country. They were, those first months upon the river, as if at play in the fields of the Lord. They had entered the Garden. Captain Clark, 23 August 1804: "I walked on Shore and killed a fat Buck."

By the time, nearly a year later, that the expedition passed the northeast corner of the Helena Valley, the members' unbridled enthusiasm had sobered. The Louisiana Purchase and the land that was to become Montana might be a garden, but it was ungodly big, most of it painfully uncultivated. Clark again, July 19, 1805: "My feet is verry much brused and cut walking over the flint and constantly stuck full of prickley pear thorns. I pulled out 17 by the light of the fire tonight. Musqutors verry troublesome."

Later, just above the headwaters of the Missouri, things also got a little hungry in the Garden. Captain Lewis:

> Nothing Killed today and our fresh meat is out. When
> we have a plenty of fresh meat I find it impossible to
> make the men take any care of it, or use it with the least
> frugallity. Tho' I expect that necessity will shortly teach
> them this art. The mountains on both sides of the river at
> no great distance are very lofty.

The mountains again, a feature which would soon play havoc with Lewis and Clark and within only a few years of their passing become home to a small but vigorous group of white ruffians known to us today as

Mountain Men. These trappers and hunters lived wild, primitive lives, and as they subdued everything in their path less wild than themselves, they also attained heroic stature in the eyes of civilized folks they had left behind. What they really did out here, of course, was live on the fat of an unspoiled land at the expense of everyone and everything in their way, leaving in their wake a legacy of death and disease. But they nonetheless became men whose skills with horse and rifle would be legendary, their lives embodying myths that often, unfortunately, overshadow the difference between the land they found and the land they left behind. We remember instead—or envision—the trappers as *individuals ennobled by their primitive contact with nature,* elevated in stature above the mortal yeomanry left sweating behind teams of mules in Missouri. And, because solitude and independence are vital parts of the Mountain Man mythology, we also tend to forget that the majority of them worked for a small number of highly exploitive companies, whose chief concern with wilderness—like most of the corporate profiteers who followed—was to extract, ruthlessly, a wealth of raw materials in exchange for profits to be spent in the East.

Even if we admit the arrogance and violence with which these gangs of professional killers approached the wilderness and its native populations, we still insist, in our imaginations at least, on glorifying qualities we know they must have had: resourcefulness, endurance, undeniable moments of courage, and above all (in the literary tradition of Fenimore Cooper's Natty Bumpo) remarkable skills with the rifle. They lived by and achieved dominance through this latest bit of technology, after all, and their ability to shoot became both part of our western mythology and identity to such a powerful extent that some Montanans still feel compelled to fire high-speed bullets into low-speed buffalo grazing out of Yellowstone Park . . . in the tradition of our mountain-man heritage, of course.

But listen to Osborne Russell and his account of a buffalo hunt near the Snake River in 1834:

I now prepared myself for the first time in my life to kill
meat for my supper with a Rifle. I had an elegant one
but had little experience in useing it, I however
approached the band of Buffaloe crawling on my hands
and knees within about 80 yards of them then raised my
body erect took aim and shot at a bull: at the crack of the
gun the Buffaloe all ran off excepting the Bull which I
had wounded, I then reloaded and shot as fast as I could
until I had driven 25 bullets at, in and about him which
was all that I had in my bullet pouch whilst the Bull still
stood apparently riveted to the spot I watched him
anxiously for half an hour in hopes of seeing him fall, but
to no purpose, I was obliged to give it up as a bad job
and retreat to our encampment without meat.

From the beginning then, an interesting set of discrepancies between
actual experience on the frontier and the way we have since chosen to
imagine that experience, has developed: a confusion of myth with history
and of legend with literal event, which although potent has little to do
with our contemporary lives in Montana. And these discrepancies between myths like the Noble Savage, the romantic primitive, or the happy
agrarian yeoman of pastoralism and the brutal realities of both the land
here and man's abuse of that land must be blamed to a large degree on
writers; writers from outside the region who wrote mountains of fiction
about experiences they had not shared and did not understand, while
striving to create emotional responses, in a distant eastern audience,
which they had not themselves earned. Certainly the worst and most
voluminous example of this kind of writing was Erastus Beadle and his
Dime Novel Series. Beadle—like the producers of the television series
"The A Team"—realized that to make money as a publisher he would
need to attract a mass audience with a standardized product. Beadle
managed to perfect a series of formulas for adventure fiction based
loosely on the romance and wilderness perils found in Fenimore Cooper's
Leatherstocking Tales. And his dozens of books, often ghost-written in as

few as three days, with such fanciful titles as *Baby Bess the Girl Gold Miner* and *Deadwood Dick's Dream,* sold like hotcakes.

Beadle's formula was, in fact, largely responsible for the transformation of one particular mountain-man figure, from inglorious hide-hunter to American hero, still remembered today as "Buffalo Bill" Cody—a character created by a distant mass medium pandering to the ignorance of a mass market. One of Beadle's most prolific writers, Prentiss Ingram, later became a staff publicity agent for Buffalo Bill, writing two hundred ostensibly factual stories about him. That Buffalo Bill in his old age became unable to distinguish between the actual events of his life and the fiction created by ghost writers *about* him foreshadowed the frailty of our collective Montana identity today.

As if to further complicate our situation, Hollywood arrived on the scene. And it was only a matter of further technological advancement from the stylized western characters of pulp novels to the stars of the Saturday-afternoon matinees who populated our childhoods with the desperate villains, melodramatic heroes, girls in distress, and peace-loving town folk of the Sixgun Romance. The formula for these B Westerns was essentially the same as Beadle's, although the horses ran even faster on film and the barrels of the hero's guns grew noticeably brighter.

On my father's ranch there's an old bunkhouse where some pretty real cowboys used to live. Before a friend and I remodeled it several years ago, 1930s vintage posters for the Cheyenne Frontier Days Rodeo, several bullet holes, and a dozen full-color movie magazine pictures still adorned the inside walls. Gene Autry hung there, wearing radon-bright blue jeans tucked into burgundy boots and a western shirt blazing with embroidered peacocks; Gene pointed a chromed sixgun off-camera while crouching beside a silver-inlaid saddle so heavy it bowed the top rails of his corral. Imagine the confusion among those men who worked for my wrangler grandfather. There they were, working cowboys and not a decent shirt among them, let alone chromed sixguns or saddles that would take a crane to move, yet hanging on their open-studded walls like mirrors were contemporary visions of what cowboys ought to be. Or could be, if they learned to sing. Of course the men who milked and rode and hayed for my grandfather understood the fiction of Gene's pose, but there was nevertheless a distance between real and ideal that almost certainly had as much to do with the Saturday-night bullet holes in the walls as the dozen or so whiskey bottles I found when I tore up the floor. And that same distance between what we experience in our routine lives in Montana today and the way that experience is reinterpreted has an awful lot to do with the writing that has lately sprung to life here, writing that resists the primitivism of mountain men, the romance of "saving the ranch," and a chivalric code that rides exclusively on horseflesh at the expense of "helpless" women.

Some time ago Wallace Stegner asserted that the West does not need to explore its myths much further. "It has already relied on them too long," he said. And of course he's right. For most of us today Montana has become a Western Twilight Zone where you can count the Minuteman missile silos as you drive the last thirty miles of gravel road to the Augusta Rodeo; where self-proclaimed mountain men snatch world-class women athletes, shoot up the posse, and retire into the wilderness to survive off the land undetected for six months; where commuting businessmen are as accustomed to seeing cowhands on horseback moving cattle in the browngrass foothills above the interstate highways as the cowboys themselves are to microwaved burritos and laser stereo discs; where our fastlane lives simply refute most of our western fantasies, whether they are inherited, mythological, or imported from Hollywood. And the contradictions between who we think we're supposed to be and who we seem to have become sometimes make us, as Tom McGuane says, "just a leetle crazy." In a place like this, dime-novel idealism just does not mix with real-life bad-time blues; at least once a month it seems somebody goes out to the parking lot for a .44 magnum Peacemaker replica in a tragic attempt to sort out his troubles the old-fashioned way.

Drugs, food-stamp lines, AIDS, and the threat of nuclear meltdowns are facts of life for Montanans who still, at least in some secret recess of their imaginations, see themselves as isolated and independent and stolid as the winter hunters, line-shack herders, and singlejack prospectors of the last century. But few of us really do those things anymore, which makes our schizophrenic situation here all the more painful and unpredictable. Fact is, a whole lot of us sell cameras down at K Mart or fry hamburgers for a living.

Amid this confusion, writers—some native to the state, others who moved in a few years back to stay, still more who migrate between here and someplace else—are today producing fiction set in Montana that focuses on this western chaos; fiction that probes our shaky sense of place and our wobbly sense of ourselves . . . our alternating lusts for open spaces and wider highways, for untamed wilderness and greater access. Writers appeared who have been crass and honest enough to write about what they really see here, wise enough, like Bill Kittredge and the late Richard Hugo, to understand and accept the desolation of small-town life and the vertigo of rural isolation; writers frank enough, like Richard Ford, to create characters whose only connection with landscape is to stare at it through the windows of an expensive, stolen car, and in no way be ennobled by the ride. There's Tom McGuane, who often drops his characters through a filter of new money into Montana towns like Livingston and lets them discover that for them there will be no enduring home in this place, no healing contact with land even if the land is right there waiting. New writers have appeared in the wings who bring more than education and a knack for words to their craft, authors like Neil McMahon, who understand the grinding weight as well as joy of working with one's back for a living, and poets like professional rodeo cowboy Paul Zarzyski who admit the pain of injury as well as the continuing passion to compete. There are even a couple of ranchers among this new bunch, although it's anybody's guess who let them in or for how long.

Many of Montana's new writers produce work that crosses traditional lines between genre fiction and "serious fiction" in settings as grand as the high Crazy Mountains and as grim as poolhall latrines. James Crumley's popular detective novels come to mind, where violence is balanced by an honest compassion for losers lost along the way, where something like love can pass between father and son on the front stoop of a country bar as well as a lesson on life's priorities. This scene, for example, from Crumley's newly rereleased novel, *The Wrong Case:*

> He came out behind me, a huge dark man smiling
> tiredly, a glass of neat whiskey in his large hand. With
> the first swallow, he rinsed out his mouth, then spit off
> the porch into the dust that rimmed the parking lot. The
> second, he drank, emptying the glass. Then he patted
> me on the head, perhaps sensing what I felt. Even at his
> drunkest, he was kind and perceptive, at least around
> me. As he held my head in his great hand, I was warm in
> the lingering sunset chill. . . . The fields, a lush, verdant
> green, grew dark with shadows, nearly as dark as the
> pine-thick ridges, but the sky above still glowed a bright,
> daylight blue. A single streak of clouds, like a long trail
> of smoke, angled away from the horizon, flaming a violet
> crimson at the far end as if it had been dipped in blood.
> But the middle was light pink and the end nearest us was
> an ashen gray.
>   "A lovely view, isn't it, son?"
>   "Yes, sir."
>   "But it's not enough," he said, smiling, then he
> walked back into the bar, laughing and shouting for
> whiskey, love, and laughter, leaving me suspended in
> the pellucid air.

Like Crumley, most contemporary Montana fiction writers concentrate on characters who ride not so much from the purple sage as from broken marriages, failed attempts to reinvent themselves, and overdue, unpayable debts. They seek not so much to tame the West as to find ways to face it. Many such characters don't make it, and what is most clear in their failures is that they are not heros, but men and women struggling as best they can with contemporary problems in an extraordinary place. Caught between the extremes of complex urban society and the emptiness of rural isolation, these characters, like many of us, yo-yo between the two, as unable to enter society for long as to return home in any lasting way. No one brings this effort and the chilling possibility of failure into sharper focus than James Welch. From his first novel, *Winter in the Blood:*

> It could have been the country, the burnt prairie
> beneath a blazing sun, the pale green of the Milk River
> valley, the milky waters of the river, the sagebrush and
> cottonwoods, the dry, cracked gumbo flats. The country
> had created a distance as deep as it was empty, and the
> people accepted and treated each other with distance.
> But the distance I felt came not from country or
> people; it came from within me. I was as distant from
> myself as a hawk from the moon.

Perhaps these prodigals are Montana's truest present characters, embodying a longing most of us share for a connectedness to place and culture, an invitation to stay, or at least an honest welcome home. And so it is, that we struggle in our literature as in our lives with the distances within us and between us in our bittersweet attempts to connect with this place Montana.

Readings

Adams, Robert, Lewis Baltz, and others. *Landscape: Theory.* New York: Lustrum Press, 1980.

Adams, Robert, *Beauty in Photography: Essays in Defense of Traditional Values.* New York: Aperture, 1981.

Adnan, Etal, and others. *Russell Chatham.* Seattle: Winn Books, 1984.

Broder, Patricia Janis. *The American West: The Modern Vision.* New York: Little, Brown, 1984.

*My sincere thanks to Bill Kittredge and Bill Bevis for plowing the ground and planting the seeds for this essay.

Goetzmann, William H., and William N. Goetzmann, *The West of the Imagination*. New York: W. W. Norton, 1986.

Heidenreich, C. Adrian and Virginia L. *Montana Landscape: One Hundred Years*. Billings, Montana: Yellowstone Art Center, 1982.

Johnstone, Mark. "Landscape: Perceiving the Land as Image" in *New Landscapes*, James Alinder, editor. Carmel, California: The Friends of Photography, 1981.

Kittredge, William. *Owning It All*. St. Paul: Graywolf Press, 1987.

Martin, Russell, and Marc Barasch. *Writers of the Purple Sage: An Anthology of Recent Western writing*. New York: Viking Penguin, 1984.

McConnell, Gordon. *A Montana Collection: 1985–1987 Recent Acquisitions by the Yellowstone Art Center*. Billings, Montana: The Yellowstone Art Center, 1987.

Stegner, Wallace, and Richard W. Etulain. *Conversations with Wallace Stegner on Western History and Literature*. Salt Lake City: University of Utah Press, 1983.

Stegner, Wallace, and Page Stegner. *American Places*. Moscow, Idaho: University of Idaho Press, 1983.

Szarkowski, John. *American Landscapes*. New York: The Museum of Modern Art, 1981.

Trenton, Patricia, and Peter H. Hassrick. *The Rocky Mountains: A Vision for Artists in the Nineteenth Century*. Norman, Oklahoma: University of Oklahoma, 1983.

Whipple, Dan. "The Meaning of Landscape: Through the Eyes of Gary Bates." *Northern Lights*, Vol. II, No. 1, January/February 1986.